Sumerian Mythology

Fascinating Sumerian History and Mesopotamian Empire and Myths

© **Copyright 2019 - All rights reserved.**

The content contained within this book may not be reproduced, duplicated or transmitted without direct written permission from the author or the publisher.

Under no circumstances will any blame or legal responsibility be held against the publisher, or author, for any damages, reparation, or monetary loss due to the information contained within this book. Either directly or indirectly.

Legal Notice:

This book is copyright protected. This book is only for personal use. You cannot amend, distribute, sell, use, quote or paraphrase any part, or the content within this book, without the consent of the author or publisher.

Disclaimer Notice:

Please note the information contained within this document is for educational and entertainment purposes only. All effort has been executed to present accurate, up to date, and reliable, complete information. No warranties of any kind are declared or implied. Readers acknowledge that the author is not engaging in the rendering of legal, financial, medical or professional advice. The content within this book has been derived from various sources. Please consult a licensed professional before attempting any techniques outlined in this book.

By reading this document, the reader agrees that under no circumstances is the author responsible for any losses, direct or indirect, which are incurred as a result of the use of information contained within this document, including, but not limited to, — errors, omissions, or inaccuracies.

Table of Contents

Table of Contents	5
Introduction	7
Chapter 1: The History of Sumer	21
Chapter 2: Sumerian Society and Religion	38
Chapter 3: Tales of Gods and Goddesses	68
Chapter 4: The Exploits of Ninurta	78
Chapter 5: Tales of Kings and Heroes	82
Chapter 6: Tales of Inanna	87
Chapter 7: Tales of Nanna	92
Chapter 8: The Epic of Gilgamesh	96
Chapter 9: Lighter Tales of Sumerian Gods and Heroes	102
Chapter 11: Twenty Essential Facts about Sumerian History and	114
Mythology	114
List of Sumerian Gods, Goddesses, and Heroes	125
Frequently Asked Questions	130
Conclusion	152

Introduction

It is believed that the people of Sumer worshipped somewhere between one hundred and three hundred gods and goddesses. Because of overlap in the geographic area, Sumerian gods and goddesses also exist in Akkadian and Babylonian mythology although the names used for these divinities are occasionally different. Sumerian mythology is little known to most people in the West at present, which serves to make the tales of the gods and heroes of this ancient region an object of fascination for those interested in mythology. And there are many people interested in the myths and legends of ancient peoples. Because the Fertile Crescent was an area with close contact with other regions, the mythology of this region was able to have a great influence on the mythologies of other including the Phoenicians and the Greeks.

Indeed, much has been said about the supposed foreign origin of Greek gods. The example most frequently given of a foreign god is that of Aphrodite, who seems to stand apart from the other gods of Mount Olympus in terms of both her origin and her cult. The goddess Aphrodite was not related to the other gods of the Greek pantheon and her lands of veneration were primarily in the Eastern fringe of Greek settlement, such as Central Asia Minor and Cyprus. In fact, it is believed today that Aphrodite came to the Greeks through trade with the

Phoenicians in early times. She was really the Phoenician goddess Ashtoreth, who actually was the Sumerian goddess Inanna (known in later times as Ishtar).

Although Inanna was only one of many goddesses in the Sumerian pantheon, she grew in importance throughout the complex history of Mesopotamia, that is, the area straddling the Tigris and Euphrates rivers in what is now Iraq. The goddess Inanna began to be prominent during the period of King Sargon, who led the Assyrian Empire, and this goddess reached the pinnacle of her fame during the time period of the Assyrian Empire when Inanna was said to be ranked higher even than Ashur, the national god of the Assyrians. The goddess's worship declined during the centuries after the birth of Christ, especially with the arrival of Islam in the 7th century AD, but it was said that this goddess was worshipped in certain hill districts as late as the 18th century of our era.

It is important to examine the story of Inanna because she represents one of those divinities who really encapsulates the spirit of religion. In this fashion, Inanna is almost like the Thor of the Sumerians. Of course, Inanna was a Sumerian goddess, but her cult was so deeply entrenched among her people that we would compare her in prominence to a Thor for the Norse or an Apollo to the Greeks. Inanna was a goddess of love and sexuality, but she was also a goddess of war and of nationalism. In a famous relief of the Akkadian period, Inanna is shown trampling a lion, which may indicate the ability of the

Sumerians and Akkadians to be victorious over their enemies (of which there were many).

Inanna the goddess was so important to the Sumerians and other peoples of the Fertile Crescent that she was a major character in one of their formative stories, that of Gilgamesh. The tale of Gilgamesh (called the Epic of Gilgamesh) is believed to be the oldest of its kind in the world, predating the Iliad and the Odyssey by about 1500 years. This tale is preserved enough that it can still be read in the basically complete form today, more than 4000 years after it was written. Inanna was an important character in this story as she was part of the motivation of the actions of Gilgamesh in the epic and was responsible for some of his travails. It has been mentioned that Inanna was the inspiration, or equivalent, of Ashtoreth in the Phoenician pantheon, but her most famous avatar was that of Astarte, Astarte, or Ishtar: a name by which she is commonly known.

As the reader will learn in *Sumerian Mythology: Fascinating Sumerian History and Mesopotamian Empire and Myths*, the presence of similar deities in different regional civilizations can result in a confusing patchwork of names and identities. For example, the god Utu was also known as Sammas, Shamash, or Utu-Shamash (the name that he will be called in this work). He was a sun god who was the twin of Inanna. As was typical in Sumerian iconography, he was shown in many ways: sometimes is an old man with a long white beard or as a disc with wings or points in cardinal directions. As Inanna was believed to bring human beings civilization, Utu-Shamash was believed to be responsible for bringing to humans laws. To make matters even worse, Utu should not be confused with Uttu, who was both a daughter and wife to Enlil.

Because Sumerian divinities often assume distinct regional characters, or their image and worship changes somewhat over time, it is important to understand a little bit about the history of the region in order to get the full flavor of the myths. This is important even if the focus of the mythology is primarily on a certain period of time, such as the Akkadian period and earlier. These are really the darkest days of mythology, where very little has been left to us other than some remaining monuments and the occasional cuneiform tablets, inscriptions that were only translated relatively recently. Of course, we do not mean that the society or civilization was dark. Indeed, Sumerian civilization was so vibrant that we might describe it as bright or golden.

This is the region that gave birth to the Assyrians, Babylonians, and even later, the Persians. This region between two great rivers has left a legacy that may seem distant today but is still powerful and close in many ways. We have already said that gods of the Sumerian pantheon entered the mythologies of other people; well, museums are filled with images of these early gods who represent one of the oldest attested religions in the history of humanity, if not the oldest.

A study of Sumerian history is an exercise in aggrandizement and unification. If one looks at this region, one comes to understand how, over time, the people of this region became united into larger and larger polities in which the characters of regional people have sometimes swept away, but often incorporated. Perhaps, this is why the Sumerians had so many deities, as many as three hundred according to some sources.

From the small city-states of Uruk, Nippur, and others, the Sumerian civilization eventually became a large empire under the Akkadians led by Sargon, and then empires under the Assyrians, Babylonians, and others. These civilizations are not so obscure or fringe as you might think. They influenced not only the religions of the Greeks and Persians, but they also influenced Judaism, and, as a result, the other Abrahamic religions of Islam and Christianity. Another of the lessons that can be taken from this story is how local city gods could become divinities with a national character who eventually spread to other regions. This presence of gods of local, civic character that we associate with the Greeks, therefore, begins more than one thousand years before the earliest twitches of

Greek civilization during the Mycenaean and Minoan periods.

But let us turn our gaze back to Inanna. In *Sumerian Mythology: Fascinating Sumerian History and Mesopotamian Empire and Myths*, you will learn about all of the important gods of the Mesopotamian pantheon, including Inanna and Utu-Shamash, but we also count Enki, Enlil, An, Ninhursag, Nanna, and others among this number. These are gods of strange names and strange practices that may take some time getting used to, but they will become more familiar in time. In *Sumerian Mythology: Fascinating Sumerian History and Mesopotamian Empire and Myths*, you will be familiarized enough with ancient, and sometimes, obscure gods to understand how their worship impacted other civilizations and may even have left a mark that stretches right up to the present time.

As you have already discovered, Inanna was not as obscure or strange as she may at first seem. Sure, she may be depicted with wings, holding odd weapons, and trampling lions and other beasts underfoot, but she was basically the same goddess whom Botticelli depicted washing up on the shores of Cyprus in a seashell: a beautiful woman with long reddish-blond curls. She was the same goddess depicted in the Venus de Milo that is today held in the Louvre. And she was the same goddess who was responsible for setting off the Trojan War by promising to give Paris the greatest prize of all: Helen of Troy.

An easy way to be introduced to Inanna and other gods is to understand the roles they played with the important heroes of the region and their legends. So we can talk about how she loved Gilgamesh and asked him to become her divine consort. Gilgamesh refuses her, and as a result, she releases the Bull of Heaven, which leads to Enkidu's demise and the subsequent tribulations of Gilgamesh as he comes face to face with his mortality.

In the first chapter, a review of the history of Sumer will be undertaken with the end of preparing the reader for the whirlwind tour that is the story of the Sumerian gods. The story of the Sumerian gods is also the tale of the Akkadian gods, Assyrian gods, Babylonian, and Phoenician gods, to say nothing of the other cultures who drew some member of their pantheon from the divinities of the old cities of Sumer. To understand mythology, you need to understand the people. And in order to understand the people, one must be exposed to the land that birthed them.

The land that birthed the Sumerians was the land of Mesopotamia: the land between two rivers. It is a startling fact of ancient civilizations that they all arose along great rivers. The Mesopotamian civilizations arose on the great plain between the Tigris and Euphrates rivers. The Egyptian civilization, of course, arose along the Nile. The earliest civilization of South Asia arose on the banks of the Indus. And the early peoples of China arose along the Yangtze rivers. Rivers were the lifeblood of early people, allowing them not only to grow the crops they needed to support a large population, but also allowing routes for trade or conquest, and providing the staging ground for startlingly unique civilizations.

In the second chapter, we will be introduced to the society of Sumer and some of the related civilizations that followed. It may seem, at first glance, that all societies must be somewhat the same. They all have kings and warriors, priests and magi, farmers, peasants, tradesmen, and townspeople, but a closer review of the early civilizations reveals that they were all unique in their own way. In Sumer, priests played an important role, especially early on. As a matter of fact, it seems to be the hallmark of Oriental civilizations that religious figures were of paramount importance, and even when kings and emperors surpassed them, they often took on a religious character. All of this and more will be explored in the second chapter in the context of the Sumerians.

At the center of Sumerian civilization was, of course, the gods and goddesses, even if the life they took on was breathed into them by their devotees. The gods of the Near East are often fascinating because they take on somewhat of a different character from corresponding divinities in Europe. In Greek,

Roman, and Norse mythology, we see gods and goddesses who resemble men and women. They wear clothes appropriate for the society, and they carry on almost as grandiose or glorified humans. But in Sumerian, Egyptian, Assyrian, and other civilizations, we see that gods can be very different from this.

We may find gods that look like humans at a cursory glance, but perhaps have the feet of a bird, lion, or other animals. They may even have the head of an animal, a motif that was very common among the Egyptians, but which also had a place among cultures like the Sumerians. These gods were not meant to be models for people or like people in some way (as the Greco-Roman gods were). These gods might be mysterious and cruel. They may be sensual or have other exaggerated characteristics. They may be terrifying. The gods and goddesses of Sumer will be introduced in the third chapter.

You will learn several of the formative myths of the civilization, such as the story of the Cosmic Births, the tale of Enki and Ninmah, the story of Enki and Ninhursag, and the tale of Enlil and Ninlil. This introduction will begin to set the tone for not only what the gods and goddesses of Sumer were like, but what the people were like. How they lived and why they lived as they did. All this and more will be undertaken in the third chapter as we embark on a discussion of the Sumerian gods and goddesses, such as Inanna, Nanna, Enlil, Anu, and others.

As with most mythologies, there were particular gods, goddesses, and characters in the Sumerian myth that straddled their societies like colossi. These leviathans of Sumer included the primary deities - namely Enlil (or Ellil), Anu, and
Enki - but also included Inanna, Adad, Ea, Ninurta, and Nergal. There were, of course, also heroes like Gilgamesh whose tales have been transmitted to us in the present. In the fourth chapter, we will begin our survey of Sumerian myth by exploring in detail the tales of some of these critical figures. We start off this quest with Ninurta, the god of war and an important member of the pantheon of Sumerian gods and goddesses.

Just as Apollo, Zeus, and Thor had their important myths that helped to shape how the civilians in their respective societies perceived the gods, themselves, and their world, so too do the tales of the Sumerians help us understand this dynamic. In the case of Ninurta, these tales include the stories of Ninurta and
Asag, but also include the story of Ninurta's return to Nippur. Ninurta will not be the only one whose legend is explored in this way. In the sixth chapter, we will learn more about Inanna, the goddess of many names. She was also Astarte, Ishtar, Ashtoreth, and later Aphrodite. It is said that there were more tales of Inanna than of any other deity of the Sumerians. Some of these tales you will learn.

But before that, we take a detour from the gods to the realm of heroes and kings. In the fifth chapter, stories of kings and heroes will be explored as it is these figures who often give a sense of the shape the society and civilization take. We see this in other mythologies, as well. So Theseus, Perseus, Heracles, and Achilles become just as important in Greek mythology as Apollo, Zeus, and Athena. Not because they were worshipped, but because their myths give us a better sense of what the people believed and how their lives were lived.

Kings and heroes were especially important in Norse myth, where many of the sagas and poems that persist to the present day are actually tales of these real-life figures: tales in which the gods are almost supporting characters in the overall drama. We will begin the survey of the Sumerian heroes with an introduction to them: who they were and how they should be interpreted. There are many kings and heroes to discuss, including mythical ones like Gilgamesh and real ones like Sargon. You will learn the story of Enmerkar in the Ensuhkesdanna and of Sargon and Ur-Zababa.

We will return to examine more closely another god: Nanna. Nanna, the god of wisdom and the moon, should not be confused with another god already mentioned, namely, Inanna or Ishtar. The similarities in names of deities of this region can lead to confusion, but a discussion of their myths will help paint a picture of distinction that will come in handy later. The journey of Nanna to Nippur is just one of several tales of this god that will be explored in the seventh chapter.

Then comes time for perhaps the weightiest chapter of Sumerian myth and legend. This is the Epic of Gilgamesh, the oldest and certainly one of the most important works of world literature. This is the tale of the exploits of the hero Gilgamesh, a man who may have served as an inspiration for Heracles and others. We have already spoken of Gilgamesh's unfortunate run-in with Inanna, but he had other trials a well. The tales of Gilgamesh and others like Enkidu and Utnapishtum will be explored in the eighth chapter. Tales of gods and heroes will continue on in the ninth chapter when we explore some other tales including the stories of Lugalbanda in the Mountain Cave, and Lugalbanda and the Anzu bird. The Anzu, a giant bird who steals the tablet of destinies, is one of the more interesting characters the reader will learn about.

By the end of the ninth chapter, the reader will certainly have developed a strong sense of the tone of the Sumerian people and their religious belief system. The Sumerians later became part of another important civilization known as the Akkadians. This is the civilization of the great King Sargon, a man whose name is believed to refer to the role he played among his people. This was one of the first major empires in the world and it certainly played a critical role in spreading

Sumerian beliefs to other neighboring regions, such as Phoenicia and Arabia. Although Akkadian civilization may be construed as a part of the larger Sumerian civilization, a closer examination of Akkad serves to complete the story of Sumer.

It is a story with enough oddities and twists and turns to delight even the most taciturn of readers. Certainly, mythological studies are not for everyone, but those readers on the fence about this subject will definitely have to put up a fight about Sumer as this civilization has plenty to interest people. If anything, you might be interested in how little you know about these mysterious Sumerian divinities and the long-dead people who worshipped them. Your journey into their world begins with gaining a deeper understanding of their history.

Chapter 1: The History of Sumer

Mesopotamia is one of the most fertile regions on Earth. It is a plain located between two rivers, the Euphrates River and the Tigris River, and it is strategically located in a region that is in Asia, but near to both Africa in Europe. Perhaps, that is why this region has not only given birth to some of the most significant civilizations in history, but it has been endlessly fought over by groups as diverse as the Egyptians, Romans, and Ottoman Turks. Mesopotamia was a land well worth possessing and many conquerors, including Alexander the Great, were well aware of it.

Most of Mesopotamia today is in the nation of Iraq, but parts of it are located also in Turkey, Syria, and a small number of other nations. And this does not include the nations immediately adjacent to Mesopotamia, regions that were long subject to both the political and cultural influence of this important region. The Greeks and Macedonians were just a few of the many peoples who recognized the importance of this region. The Seleucids who came to power after the death of Alexander founded their capital of Seleucia on the Tigris in

Mesopotamia. They knew that not only was the fertile plain around the city fruitful, but it provided the perfect watchtower of sorts to survey the Persians, Bactrians, and others who were anxious to rebel and gain their independence.

In this chapter, we will review the history of Mesopotamia, focusing on the Sumerian period. because the Sumerian gods also appeared in the pantheons of other civilizations in the region, we will also discuss some of the other empires that rose and fell after the earlier Sumerian and Akkadian states. The most important fact to get out of the way at once is to mention that most historians consider Mesopotamia to be the birthplace of civilizations. The earliest evidence of writing and civic living (to date) is to be found not in Egypt, not in Europe, but in Mesopotamia.

It is believed that Mesopotamia has been inhabited for at least 12,000 years. Its climate, suitableness for agriculture, and ample supply of fresh and clean water made it perfect for the formation of a civilization. As you will soon learn, the first cities of the region blossomed about 6000 years ago.

Brief Review of Mesopotamian History

Mesopotamia was a land of competing city-states during the period of 4000 BC to about 3000 BC. These cities would eventually be unified under King Sargon of the Akkadian

Empire. They would continue to be united under the overlordship of the Assyrians and the Babylonians. The region was notable for almost constant warfare, which did not prevent great agricultural advancements and a state of high civilization from developing. The scale of the building was massive in Mesopotamia, including the ziggurats, buildings designed to allow for communication with the Sumerian gods.

The people of Mesopotamia were notable not only for their agriculture and religious practices but for their advancements in math and science. Some of the practices developed during this time are taken for granted today. These mathematical advancements included the sixty-second minute, the sixtyminute hour, and the circle made up of three hundred and sixty degrees. One of the major applications of such mathematical practices was astronomy.

The Babylonians, for example, divided the year into twelve periods. Each period was given the name of the most prominent constellation in the night sky, essentially a zodiac system that is still used in some religions and cultures today. The seven-day week is something else that can be laid at the feet of the Babylonians. The most important advancement of the people of Mesopotamia, however, is believed to be the system of writing.

This system began as pictographs, not unlike the hieroglyphics of the Ancient Egyptians. This system would eventually develop into what we know today as writing. This writing system began to appear by about 3200 BC. Today we call it cuneiform. It was so flexible that it would become the basis for more than one dozen languages including Babylonian, Hittite, Persian, and Elamite. Hammurabi's Code, the oldest law code of its kind, was written in the cuneiform that the people of Mesopotamia developed.

Mesopotamia's riches, both material and intellectual, would eventually be the cause of its downfall. Cities like Babylon were just too attractive to foreigners to be overlooked as a target for conquest. Beginning with the conquest of Babylon by the Persians in 539 BC, Mesopotamia would find itself in the hands of foreigners. Mesopotamia would fall into the rank of second-rate nations under the control of others. Its city would disappear into the sands, but its legacy of science, language, and mathematics would remain right up to the present.

The Sumerians

It is believed by some that the transition from huntergathering societies to large agricultural societies occurred in Mesopotamia sometime between 10,000 BC and 4000 BC. In Sumerian civilization, we find the earliest documented evidence of the wheel, astronomy, language, and the division of time. The first true cities are also developed in Sumer, a region in Southern Mesopotamia.

The earliest citied belonged to the Ubaid Culture of Sumer, which lasted from about 6000 BC to about 4000 BC. Waves of migration occurred from the coastal regions to the West, in modern-day Syria, into the Mesopotamian plains. The Sumerian culture was formed through the interaction of these cities. The cities of Sumer included Kish, Ur, Eridu, Nippur, Uruk, and Babylon. Because there was a food surplus produced by these cities, much of the population was able to devote itself to other activities which allowed the advancements of Mesopotamia that were previously mentioned.

These great cities of Sumer formed rivalries with one another and attracted outsiders. The first walled cities were created at sites such as Uruk. Eventually, all of the major cities of Sumer had walls. In about 2500 BC, Enshakushanna, king of Uruk, conquered most of the city-states of Sumer and declared himself "Lord of Sumer." His rule was brief as a rival king would conquer Uruk as well as the former city-states that were dependent upon Uruk. During this time, Sumerian kings conquered the neighboring Kingdom of Mari and even had conquest in the East at the Elamite city of Susa.

About one hundred years later, a man from Kish rose from the status of cupbearer to conquer the cities of Kish and Uruk. This was Sargon, the founder of Akkad. This period in Sumerian history was one of assimilation. This became important in Sumerian history as city-states had distinct identities as virtual nations, and Sargon allowed Sumer and Akkad to develop an identity as a unified Mesopotamian nation.

The Akkadians

Sargon's ambitions did not end once he had unified the cities of Sumer in southern Mesopotamia. He went on to conquer all the cities and other places on the fertile plain of Mesopotamia. He founded an empire; in fact, the empire of Sargon is believed by many historians to have been the first in world history. It was an empire because Sargon ruled people who spoke different languages and had their own separate bureaucratic institutions.

During his time, the native language of the Sumerians was replaced with a script of Semitic origins (i.e. from the Eastern Mediterranean to the West of Sumer). His state became known as the Akkadian Empire and it would last under the descendants of Sargon for nearly two hundred years. During this time, a state to the east of Sumer called Susa would rise to prominence. The Susans would become strong enough and developed enough to challenge the Akkadians for influence in the region.

This time period also saw the rise of the Gutian people as a challenge to the Akkadians. The Gutians would attack the Akkadians leading to the slow erosion of the Akkadian Empire. They would burn Akkad, the capital city of the Akkadians to the ground. The location of Akkad remains a mystery, although historians and archaeologists have used documentary evidence from the period and later to get a general idea of where the city might be. Many believe it to be very near to the city of Baghdad, which is the capital of the modern nation of Iraq.

The Akkadians would be replaced politically in the region by the so-called Neo-Sumerian Empire, which is also known as the Third Dynasty of Ur. This period of the Neo-Sumerian Empire would last from about 2100 BC to about 2000 BC. This period would come to an end because of the deprecations of the Amorites, an Arabian tribe to the south who were just then growing in prominence. The Amorites would adopt much of the religion and culture of the Neo-Sumerians, and they would make their capital at Babylon. Babylon would eventually become one of the most famous cities in the world.

One last important fact to note about the Akkadian and NeoSumerian period is what historians refer to as the widespread bilingualism of the period. During this time, although Akkadian was in some ways replacing Sumerian administratively, the populace was largely bilingual in both Akkadian and Sumerian. It would not be until the Amorite period that Akkadian decisively replaced Sumerian as both an administrative and a spoken language in Mesopotamia.

Evidence for the importance of Akkadian can be seen in the names of the kings of major cities like Assur and Eshnunna. Currently, the center of religious activity was the important city of Nippur. In this city, Enlil was the major divinity. Enlil would remain the supreme deity of Sumer until the rise of Babylon in the 18th century BC. It would be the Amorites and one of their kings, Hammurabi, who would be responsible for the rise of Babylon as a major city.

The Amorites and Amurru

There has been much confusion and misinformation surrounding the Amorites. Racial theorists of the 19th and early 20th centuries claimed that the Amorites were Aryans who were distinct from the other peoples of the region. They came to this conclusion because of the description that has been passed down through the ages, specifically that the Amorites were tall. Some even claimed that King David and Jesus were "Aryan" Amorites, even though there was no evidence to corroborate this assertion. Today, historians understand that the Amorites were a clearly Semitic people who perhaps were identical to the Canaanites who dwelled in the region of the Southern Levant before the arrival of the Jews from Egypt.

Amurru is the name given for both a specific people (who we now know today as the Amorites) and for the god that they worship. This god was also called Martu, and his important city was called Ninab. Like many other cities of the region, the precise location of this city is not known to historians and archaeologists. Amurru and Martu are documented in texts in both the Akkadian and Sumerian languages.

Amurru was regarded as the god of the Amorite people. The Amorites were originally a tribal, uncivilized people who lived on the fringe of the Akkadian and Neo-Sumerian empires. They were pastoral and they were often referred to as people of the mountain or of the steppe. For this reason, Amurru (the god) was also referred to as lord of the mountain or lord of the steppe. As lord of the mountain, Amurru was called Bel Sade, which means the same. This has led to some confusion among scholars as the god of Abraham was also called Bel Sade (lord of the mountain). Some believed that this god developed into the infamous god of the Bible, Baal.

Although not much attention has been placed on the gods of the region as of yet, this is a good juncture to begin the discussion of one. Although Amurru technically was not a god of rigidly Sumerian origins, because the Amorites conquered Mesopotamia and made the peripheral city of Babylon their capital, Amurru began to be a god that the Sumerian people of Mesopotamia worshipped, and therefore is counted among Sumerian gods today (of which there are said to be as many as three hundred). Amurru is often depicted as a shepherd or a storm-god. The existence of Amurru points to the duality of gods in Sumerian history and culture. This was a regional god who became adopted into the scores of gods that were worshipped by the people of Mesopotamia. Gods, therefore, had a dual role as both divinities of particular places or peoples where they were originally worshipped and larger deities of empires and wider nationalities. This duality that is very remarkable in the Mesopotamians is also seen to a degree in the Greeks with their civic fondness for this deity or that.

The Assyrians

The Assyrians are one of the few people discussed in this book who continue to exist in the present. The Assyrians are regarded as a group native to the Middle East. Today, these people are also known as Syriacs, Chaldeans, and Arameans. They live primarily in Northern Iraq, Turkey, and Eastern Syria, regions which are regarded as their homeland and which constituted the central regions of the Assyrian Empire.

Today, most Assyrians are Christian but in the past, they would have worshipped gods similar to those worshipped by their Mesopotamian neighbors.

The Assyrian Empire and its people take their name from the city of Assur. This was an important city especially in the Akkadian period and the centuries immediately preceding it. Kist of Assyrian kings from this very early period remain. Most of them would have been local potentates ruling as vassals under an Akkadian or Neo-Sumerian king. The Assyrian cities of Assur and Nineveh are attested as early as 2500 BC, although they were not independent city-states at this time.

The Assyrian period is broken up into parts based on the times of independence and empire for the Assyrians. The earliest period of statehood was known as the Early Assyrian Period, although the first major period of the empire was the Old Assyrian Empire. During this time, the Assyrian state ruled the entire Mesopotamian region, which natives of the area knew as the four corners of the world. Their state was bordered by the Zagros Mountains to the East, the Caucasus Mountains in the North, the Arabian Desert in the South, and the Mediterranean Sea to the West.

The original capital of this state was the city of Assur, although other, later capitals included Shubat-Enlil and Nineveh. The first ruled of the Old Assyrian Empire was Puzur-Ashur I, and he was followed by many great rulers over a period of more than six hundred years. The bilingualism of the Sumerians during the preceding period has already been discussed. During the Assyrian Empire, the Assyrians spoke a dialect of the Akkadian language. Their inscriptions were written in a script that was known as Old Assyrian.

The Assyrians were followers of the polytheistic Mesopotamian religion. At the center of the Assyrian pantheon was their national god, Assur (or Ashur), who, like Amurru for the Amorites, shared the same name as the people. It is a strange similarity that this sharing of a name is also seen in the city of Athens where Athena was worshipped. The other gods in the Assyrian pantheon included Adad, Ninurta, Ninlil, Nergal, Sin, and Ishtar (or Inanna).

The Old Assyrian Empire may have been the first major period of the Assyrian state, but it was not the only one. There was also the Middle Assyrian Empire, which lasted from about 1400 BC to about 900 BC, and the Neo-Assyrian Empire, which occurred from about 900 BC to about 600 BC.

The Babylonians

During much of the Assyrian period, Babylon was an important center that gradually rose in prominence to become one of the most important cities of the region. Like the

Assyrians, there were several periods in which the Babylonian state existed as an important regional power and even an empire. The situation becomes confused in the period of about 2000 BC to 1300 BC as there were several major states in the region vying for influence, namely the Old Assyrian Empire and the First Babylonian Dynasty.

The First Babylonian Dynasty was important mainly because one of its rulers was one of the most famous in history, Hammurabi. As has already been stated, Hammurabi was an Amorite who was known because of the code of laws which he left. The Amorites had come from the Levantine coast to establish themselves as rulers in Mesopotamia, including the regions that were earlier known as Sumer and Akkad. The First Babylonian Dynasty lasted from about 1900 BC to about 1600 BC. This first dynasty began to decline quickly after the death of Hammurabi. it split into various states and the northern part was overrun. Eventually, the city of Babylon itself was sacked by the Hittites, a significant people whose state lay primarily in Turkey. The Hittites were also known for defeating the Egyptians in battle. The Egyptians knew them as the Hyksos, and they were important for ending the Middle Period of Egyptian history, which eventually led to an Egyptian golden age under the New Period. The exact date of the sack of Babylon is not known, but it has been dated somewhere between 1499 BC and 1736 BC.

Because Babylon was so centrally located, it became a part of many other empires and states in the region. The period of disintegration was followed by three important periods centered on Babylon. These were the Kassite Period, the Iron Age Period, and the Neo-Babylonian Empire. This last period is also known as the Chaldean Period, and it lasted from about 620 BC to about 539 BC. This period is most famous because it was extensively mentioned in the Old Testament of the Bible.

The Chaldean or Neo-Babylonian Empire was the state of King Nebuchadnezzar. The Bible calls him" the destroyer of nations," and it was in this period that Daniel was thrown into the lion's den according to the Holy Book.

The Phoenicians

The Phoenicians were among the most important peoples in the region, even though they technically did not live in Mesopotamia. Their coastal cities are located primarily in the modern region of Lebanon, known even in ancient time for its fragrant cedarwood. The city-state model was very important in ancient times, and Phoenicia was a land of city-states more so than of national empire.

Although the Phoenicians may seem peripheral to the story of Mesopotamia and the Sumerians, they were essential in transmitting much of Sumerian life and culture to people outside the Near East, namely the Greeks. We have already seen that at least one goddess in the Greek pantheon was of Near Eastern origin. This was Aphrodite, who originates with the Phoenician goddess Ashtoreth. Ashtoreth is herself derived from the Sumerian goddess Inanna or Ishtar.

Although Aphrodite of the Greeks was denuded of all the foreign accouterments that characterized Inanna/Ishtar/Ashtoreth, she still stands out as a white elephant among the Olympians. Her sensual nature, magnetism, and virtual independence from men clearly indicate that she was of both a non-Greek and pre-Greek origin. Aphrodite not only neglects and steps out on her husband, Hephaestus, but she develops a character stronger than many of the other Greek gods because her worship retains its non-Greek character. Indeed, goddesses like Athena and Aphrodite embody the religion of the Sumerians perhaps more than the other Greek gods. Although historians of today associate the invaders who settled in Greece in the 2nd millennia and later as patriarchal people obsessed with sky gods, it is rather significant that not all of the gods introduced during this period were male.

Although not all of the gods of the Phoenicians made their way to the Greeks, the Phoenician influence was still felt. Even the Greek alphabet was inspired by the Phoenician alphabet.

Phoenician was a Semitic language that was related to other members of the Semitic language family. The Phoenicians had a distinct pantheon of gods, but they adhered to the overall Mesopotamian trend of worshipping a wide cadre of gods, many of whom originated from outside of their own country.

Phoenicia was important historically because its cities like Tyre and Biblos were important for founding cities like Carthage, which became one of the most significant empires in the Mediterranean before the rise of Rome.

The Persians

Although the Phoenicians were very influential in world history, it would be the Persians who would finally end the Babylonian independence of the Neo-Babylonian or Chaldean period. Even the Bible speaks of the arrival of the Persians, which would change the history of the region forever. With the arrival of the Persians, Mesopotamia would no longer be the center of the empire, but an emporium within other larger and more important states.

The Persians formed the largest empire ever seen up to that point. They ruled from the deserts of the East to the mountains of Europe to the West. They ruled also much of Northern Africa, namely Egypt which had the prestige of being one of the longest-lasting and wealthiest states in world history. The Persians had their own gods, so with their arrival, the Mesopotamian gods saw the beginning of their end. The Persian Empire would be followed by the Empire of Alexander, which would be followed by the Seleucid Empire. The

Seleucids would be followed by the Parthians who, in turn, would be followed by the Sassanians. The Sassanians were the last major state in the region before the arrival of Islam, though by this time, the flame of the Mesopotamian gods had already almost gone out.

Chapter 2: Sumerian Society and Religion

The Sumerians have left a lasting legacy in the form of language, astronomy, and mathematics. They are the civilization which we today are most removed from in terms of time, but in terms of our life today, we owe quite a bit to these inhabitants of the fertile plain of Mesopotamia. As we have seen, language, astronomy, and mathematics are just a few of the things we owe to the Sumerians. The existence of a largescale civilization was made possible by advancements in agriculture. This freed the populace to engage in other activities and made the creation of a language essential. If it were not for this early civilization, we might still be living as hunter-gatherers today.

Sumerian Society

Sumerian society, even the relatively small bit that is known to us, was extremely old. It could be dated as early as 4500 BC, making it about one thousand years older than the nearest major civilization in both geographic area and time: the

Egyptians. Although we date the formation of Sumerian society this far back in time, the cuneiform records only go back to about 3000 BC.

The Sumerians had an elaborate polytheistic religion. Their deities were anthropomorphic, which means they had characteristics of animals as well as human beings. They represented the forces at work in the world and the universe. Therefore, these gods had a cosmic significance. The earliest literature of the Sumerians identifies four major gods: Enlil, Enki, An, and Ninhursag. Just as in Norse and Greek mythology, the gods were not always well-behaved. They were mischievous, even towards one another. It seemed that the idea of the gods being somehow like humans, even in their negative qualities, persisted right up until the decline of polytheism thousands of years later.

Sumerian society was always based on civic life, but it is believed to have become more urbanized around 3000 BC, which is around the time that the earliest records were created. The urban nature of society at this time caused the gods to be identified with cities. The Sumerians essentially lived in what we would call city-states, and each city had their patron deity. The patron deity was believed by the people to be the special protector of the city and its people. There were a very large number of divinities at this time, and their relationship to the cities has been studied using information from cuneiform tablets.

The single greatest change to Sumerian society occurred when Sumer was conquered by the Akkadians. The Akkadians lived immediately to the north of Sumer proper. As a result of the conquest of Sumer by the Akkadians, the Akkadian language (a Semitic language) began to be used alongside Sumerian. The Akkadian gods became syncretized, or combined, with the old gods of Sumer. Sumerian society became more feudal, and the people saw their gods as living in a feudal order much as the people did. The chief god at this time was Enlil, from whom Enki and Inanna derived their power.

Sumerian Religion

The Sumerians believed that the world was a giant dome that was enveloped in a primordial sea. The earth was the base of the dome, and beneath this exited both an underworld and an ocean of fresh water (as opposed to the primordial saltwater sea). The deity of the dome-shaped heavens was An. An was believed to be the ancestor of the gods, who were collectively known as Anunna, which simply meant the offspring of An (or Anu).

The Sumerians believed in an afterlife. To them, the afterlife was a dark cavern that was located far below the ground of the earth. There, people that had died lived a version of the life they had lived on earth, but in the shadows. The underworld was known as Kur and it was presided over by a goddess called Ereshkigal. Everyone who died went to the afterlife, but their treatment there was not depended on their actions when they were alive. It is believed that Ereshkigal may have been an inspiration for the Greek goddess Hecate. At the very least, Hecate was regarded as the Greek equivalent of the much older Ereshkigal.

In this chapter, we will be introduced to the Sumerian religion by reviewing the major gods of the Sumerian pantheon. In cases where the god has another Akkadian, Assyrian, or Babylonian name by which they are sometimes known in modern literature, this name will be given. We begin our review with Enlil, the most important of the gods in the Akkadian period.

Enlil (or Ellil)

Enlil was called the Great Mountain, Lord of the Wind, and Father of the Gods. Enlil was not only worshipped by the people of Sumer. This god also came to be worshipped by the Akkadians, Assyrians, Hurrians, and Babylonians. The Hurrians lived in Northern Iraq and Turkey and were also known as Mitanni. The Hurrians were closely associated with the Hittites and were a population group within the large Hittites. It is believed that Armenians are an amalgamation of Hurrians with Indo-European peoples of the region.

But back to Enlil. Enlil was worshipped all over the Sumerian world. His chief place of worship was in the city of Nippur where he had a holy place called the Ekur temple. It was believed that this temple had been built by Enlil himself. The temple was believed to anchor heaven to earth. It was said that Enlil was so sacred that not even the other gods could look upon his face. As is the case with other Sumerian divinities, Enlil experienced an increase in prominence due to the rise in importance of his city of devotion, Nippur. Nippur began to rise around 2400 BC, during the Akkadian period. Enlil continued to be worshipped for centuries, although he was eventually replaced in Mesopotamia by the Babylonian god Marduk. Bel, a Babylonian god, was a deity resulting from the syncretism of Marduk, Enlil, and Dumuzid.

An (or Anu)

An, later known as Anu, was the god of the sky. An was sort of the Zeus of the Sumerian pantheon, although he was not always the chief deity, being replaced during most of the Sumerian period by Enlil. An was the ancestor of the deities in the Sumerian pantheon. For example, Enlil was a son of Anu and Ki. Enki was also a son of Anu by Nammu. Many of these children of Anu went on to father children of their own. For example, Enki was the father of Ninsar, Ninti, Ninkurra, and Uttu.

Anu had three consorts, although they are associated with different periods in Sumerian history. His consorts were Uras, and later Ki and Antu. Antu is merely the female form of the name An or Anu. Anu appears in the Epic of Gilgamesh when Inanna or Ishtar, his daughter, cajoles her father into allowing her to use the Bull of Heaven to attack the hero Gilgamesh. Anu's center of worship was in the important city of Uruk where his Eanna temple was located. Anu would later cede his patron status of Uruk to Inanna, signaling the gradual decline of Anu as one of the chief gods of Sumer.

Enki

Enki was the god of wisdom, water, and creation. He was the ruler of the Earth. This god was also known as Ea in the myths of the Akkadians and Babylonians. Like the other gods, Enki was originally a regional god who later acquired a national status. The cult of this god spread far outside the borders of Sumer and Akkad. Enki was worshipped by the Hittites, Hurrians, and Canaanites. Enki was unusual in that he was sometimes referred to in tablets by a number - the number 40

- which became his sacred number. Enki was associated with Mercury, the planet. In Babylonian times, the god Nabu, son of the important god Marduk, became associated with Enki as part of the ongoing process of syncretism.

Enki was very frequently mentioned in Sumerian myths. Myths about Enki came from all over the Mesopotamian world, attesting to his wide worship. Enki was also worshipped for a very prolonged period. His worship is attested from about 3000 BC all the way down to the Seleucid Empire of the Hellenistic Age. It is not clear what the name Enki means, but the words En and Ki are believed to mean "lord" and "earth." Enki's shrine was at Eridu, where some believe he was originally known as Ea, which means "lord of water." This has caused confusion as Ea is generally believed to be a later name for Enki possibly derived from the Hurrians. Enki later was regarded as the lover of Ninhursag.

Other Deities:

Adad

Adad was a god of storms. This god was originally Semitic but was introduced to the Mesopotamians at a later date. Adad, originally known in Syria as Hadda, was brought to

Mesopotamia by the Levantine Amorites. He became an Akkadian god. This god was sometimes known as Ba'al, a name familiar from the Bible, but there were other gods that were also known by this name, so Adad should not be taken to be equivalent to the god Ba'al.

Adad was also a rain god. He was identified with the bull, and in terms of iconography, Adad was usually depicted as bearded. He wore a bull-horned headdress and sported a thunderbolt and club in his hands. Some have suggested that Adad was the Babylonian equivalent of Zeus because of his association with the sky, thunder, and storms. This would make Adad also the Babylonian-Akkadian equivalent of Jupiter. Other gods who correspond to Adad would be Teshub, the storm god of the Hittites, and Amun, a god of the Egyptians.

Amurru

We have already been introduced to Amurru as the patron god of the Amorites who came to Mesopotamia from the Levant. Amurru was a god of nomads. Amurru was the son of Anu, the god of the sky. Amurru was mentioned as a shepherd and was associated with mountains. There does seem to be some overlap in the Mesopotamian gods, and Amurru is an example of this situation. Amurru has some qualities of Adad, sometimes being described as a sky god or storm-bringer like Adad. Sometimes, Amurru is even referred to as the Adad of the deluge, referring to his ability to bring storms.

Amurru may be a variation of the Semitic god El. One reason this relationship is suspected is that Amurru's wife is typically Asratum, who is the wife of the god El in Hittite and Semitic tradition. The connection of Amurru to Abraham and Isaac has already been mentioned. The tie here is references of Amurru as Bel Sade. Amurru is another god that is referred to as Ba'al or lord, creating enduring confusion regarding this latter god.

Anzu

Anzu was a giant bird who stole the Tablet of Destinies. Anzu is generally regarded as a lesser deity, although there are many monuments depicting him. The origins of Anzu are not entirely clear. Some have him birthed by the fresh waters of the Apsu ocean while others place him as a son of Siris, a goddess who was a patroness of beer. Anzu's iconography shows him as a fire-breathing bird. In a well-known relief, the god Ninurta is shown pursuing Anzu after this latter god steals the Tablet of Destinies.

Anzu is not mentioned as often in mythology as are some other characters. He is usually associated with the theft of the clay tablet known as the Tablet of Destinies. These tablets were either held by Enki or Enlil. Interestingly, Anzu is actually known as Indugud in Sumerian cuneiform remains. Anzu is the Akkadian name for the bird god. The Tablet of Destinies was stolen because whoever possessed this tablet could supposedly control the universe. The oldest version of the myth of the theft of this tablet placed the hero as Ningusu, while the more familiar version of the story gives the hero as Ninurta.

Apkallu

Apkallu is the name of sages or wise men of Babylonian myth. Historians describe these Apkallu today as seven demigods who possess great wisdom. These Seven Sages, as they are often known, have anthropomorphic qualities. They are usually described as being part fish and part man. After the deluge of the Epic of Gilgamesh, the sages are sometimes described as being human rather than as gods or demigods. The term Apkallu does not have to refer to the specific Seven Sages of certain myths. Kings, gods, or other rulers can also be called by this name as an indication of the great wisdom or cleverness that the individual possesses. The name Apkallu, as an epithet, literally means "the wise."

Ashur

Ashur was the main god of the Assyrian people. Ashur's iconography sometimes shows him riding a snake. Ashur, the god, should not be confused with another Ashur who was a character from Biblical stories. Ashur was also known as Assur, which tied him closely to the Assyrian people. Iconography from Mesopotamia sometimes uses a figure known as the feather-robed archer, and Ashur is often displayed in this guise.

In terms of this god's role, Ashur the god was believed to be the deified version of the city. Ashur eventually was identified with Enlil, the chief god of the Akkadian pantheon. With the rise of this identification, Ashur was given a family. He took on Enlil's wife Ninlil, who became known as Mulissu to the Assyrians, and he was given sons Zababa and Ninurta. This identification of Ashur with a wife and sons began about one thousand years after Ashur's beginnings in about 2500 BC. Under the Assyrians, Ashur was the head of the Babylonian pantheon. His name at this time was written with the cuneiform symbols which meant "whole heaven."

Bull of Heaven

The Bull of Heaven is a character who appears in the Epic of Gilgamesh. The Bull of Heaven is slightly different in the

Akkadian Epic of Gilgamesh than he is in the earlier poem of Sumer. The story of the Bull of Heaven centers around Gilgamesh's rejection of the goddess Inanna, or Ishtar. Inanna then asks her father for the Bull of Heaven so that she can send it against the hero Gilgamesh. Anu agrees to give his daughter the Bull of Heaven, which is then sent by Inanna against Gilgamesh and his friend Enkidu. Enkidu and Gilgamesh together slay the Bull of Heaven.

But the twain was not done with the bull or with Inanna. Enkidu tosses the thigh of the Bull of Heaven at Inanna as a taunt. The gods of the pantheon condemn Enkidu to die, which teaches Gilgamesh to fear his own demise. This device is the primary motivation for the rest of the events of the epic. In the night sky, the Bull of Heaven was identified with Taurus. Some believe that the tale of the Bull of Heaven is related to other stories of the Near East and Mediterranean world.

Dumuzid

Dumuzid, also known as Tammuz, was the consort of the important goddess Inanna. There are many reliefs of Sumer which depict the marriage of Inanna and Dumuzid. Dumuzid lived in heaven as the consort of the Queen of Heaven as Inanna came to be known. Inanna was a fertility god who also was the protector of shepherds. Dumuzid is interesting because he is described as a pre-Deluge king of a city called Bad-tibira. He is also said to be the king of the city of Uruk in the Sumerian king lists.

Inanna did not give her hand to Dumuzid without a fight. Dumuzid had to compete against a farmer named Enkimdu for the hand of Inanna. When Dumuzid makes the mistake of failing to properly mourn the death of Inanna, Ubabba returns and allows demons to drag him down to the underworld as a replacement for her. Eventually, Inanna takes back her decision and Dumuzid only has to remain in the underworld half the year, which leads to the division of the year into distinct seasons.

Ea

God of the waters upon which Earth is floating. Another name for Enki.

Ereshkigal

Ereshkigal was the goddess of the underworld. Ereshkigal was the older sister of the goddess Inanna. While Inanna is the Queen of Heaven, Ereshkigal is the Queen of the Underworld, which was called Irkalia or Kur. There are many myths told about Ereshkigal, but one is particularly significant. At one time, Inanna descended down into the underworld to increase her powers in that place. Inanna demands to be let in, but Ereshkigal tells her gatekeeper to only open the seven gates of the underworld individually after Inanna has removed seven articles of clothing. Inanna enters the domain of Ereshkigal naked, powerless to fight against her sister. Ereshkigal was married to Nergal and was the mother of Namtar, Ninazu, and Nungal.

Gula

Gula, or Nintinugga, was the goddess of doctors and healing. She was the consort of the god Ninurta. Nintinugga was the name of this divinity in Akkadian and Babylonian while Gula was a later name of the Mesopotamian region. There were many other names for this divinity as well. She was known as Balati or Belet. She was also known as Bau and Azugallatu, which means the "great healer." Nin-dindug, Ga-tun-dug, Nin Ezen, and Nin-Karrak are just some of the other names for this deity.

Gula had a number of myths and stories associated with her cult. It was said that she helped breathe the breath of life back into humanity after the deluge. She was a healer and it was Gula who helped heal mankind of the ravages of the Great

Flood. Like other Sumerian and Babylonian gods, Gula had a sort of dual nature. She was prayed to for healing purposes, but she was also prayed to punish those that harm others. Her city was Lagash, although her cult was also important at Nippur and Shirgula. Although Ninurta was her consort and she was occasionally invoked along with him, she was also invoked alone as an important deity in her own right.

Lamassu

Lamassu was an important protective deity in the religion of the Mesopotamian region, especially the Assyrians. Lamassu was depicted as a bull or lion with a human head. The iconography of Lamassu is very well-known to those who are familiar with Assyrian art and architecture. Indeed, this image of an animal's body with a crowned human head that has a benign expression is very distinctive for the Assyrian Empire. Sometimes, Lamassu is presented as a female deity, but usually, it is male. Lamassus also often had bird wings, as well.

The Lamassu and Shedu were protective divinities to the Babylonians. Lamassus also spread to neighboring regions as the image of a lion with wings and a human head is also found in Persia, especially at the massive remains in Persepolis. The

Lamassu were often shown at the entrances to palaces and temples as they acquired the traits of royal protectors later in the history of Mesopotamia. The Lamassu encompasses all life within him and gigantic sculptures of Lamassu might also grace an entrance to an important city like Babylon, Nineveh, or Assur.

Inanna or Ishtar

Inanna, also known as Ishtar, was a goddess of love, war, and fertility. Inanna is interesting because she seemed to increase in importance throughout the thousands of years of Mesopotamian civilization. She went from being one of several gods in the Sumerian pantheon to the Queen of Heaven. This made her more important in some places than even Enlil, An, and Enki. As we have seen, there were many myths and legends told of Inanna, cementing her place is one of the more significant figures in the myth of the region. She was also frequently depicted in art, though in her guise as ruler of heaven, she is sometimes confused with her elder sister Ereshkigal, who was the ruler of Kur, the cold underworld.

Inanna was also known as Ishtar. As the reader has learned, there were even more names to describe this important goddess of love. It is interesting to ponder why a love goddess has an important place in some mythologies and not in others.

It seems a characteristic of the East and Near East that such a divinity has an important role, while they seem to be less significant in Europe and other societies associated with rigid patriarchy.

The existence of Inanna in Mesopotamia does lend credence to the academic idea that the early gods of the Greeks were primarily feminine while invaders from the North, like the Dorians, brought the more masculine gods. That being said, it is important to remember that Aphrodite (who was based on Ashtoreth/Inanna) did not originate from the Greeks, but came to them through contact with the Phoenicians. Inanna was one of the longest-lived gods, her worship lasting into the Christian and even the Muslim period.

Lama

Lama is another name for the Lamassu. Lama was usually regarded as female. She was a goddess of personal or private protection.

Lamashtu

Lamashtu was a demon that preys on children. She has also been described as a monster or maleficent goddess who plagues women while they are in childbirth. She sometimes even kidnapped the children of women while they were nursing. Many evil deeds were attributed to this goddess or demigoddess including gnawing on children's bones and sucking their blood. Like many of the other Mesopotamian gods and goddesses, Lamashtu was a daughter of the sky god Anu (or An).

The iconography of Lamashtu was no less frightening than her supposed deeds. Lamashtu was depicted as having the head of a lioness, the ears and teeth of a donkey, a body covered in hair, long fingernails and fingers, and bird's feet with prominent talons. She seems to have the characteristics of a harpy in Greek myth although the deeds attributed to Lamashtu were much worse and she was greatly feared. Lamashtu was sometimes shown standing upon the back of a donkey and holding numbers of snakes. She was also commonly shown nursing animals, especially a dog or a pig. Some regard Lamashtu as bearing similarity to or overlapping with another character from the region: Lilith.

Rituals were performed to protect people from Lamashtu. The people needing protection would be women in childbirth or children that were sick. The rituals were quite involved. A figurine resembling Lamashtu was required in the ritual. The figurine was placed beside the bed of the person needing protection. The bread was offered to this figurine. A black dog had to carry the figurine and in the mouth of the figurine was placed a piglet's heart. The figurine had to be placed near the head of the individual needing protecting or to be cured for three days. On the third day, at dusk, the figurine was taken from where it rests and buried near the wall of the house.

Marduk

Marduk is regarded by scholars as a relatively late entrant into the pantheon of Mesopotamian gods. Marduk, who was known in earlier times as Marutuk, was the protector god of Babylon.
The rise of Babylon during the time of Hammurabi caused Marduk to go from regional importance to national importance in Mesopotamia. Marduk was regarded as the head divinity in the Babylonian pantheon as contrasted with the earlier strictly Sumerian or Akkadian pantheons.

Marduk's name was believed to mean the son of Utu who was immortal. Utu was the patron god of the city of Sippar, which has led some to suggest that Marduk, or Marutuk, originated here and not in Babylon. Although not all patron deities had specific roles in the pantheon, Marduk did. He was associated with water and vegetation as well as judgment. Of course, Marduk would not be the head of the Babylonian gods if he did not have an association with magic. Marduk was married to a goddess called Sarpanit. He was the heir of Anu, but the son of Ea (or Enki) and Damkina. Marduk's temple in Babylon was known as Esagila. Marduk's Mjolnir of sorts as called Imhullu.

Mushhushshu

The Mushhushshu (also Mushkhushshu or Mushussu) was a furious snake or dragon that served as protector of the other gods of the Sumerian pantheon. The Mushussu was famously depicted on the Ishtar Gate into the city of Babylon. This was a creature with a highly singular appearance. It had hind legs that resembled the talons of a bird but had the forelegs of a cat or other feline creature. It had a long neck upon which was a snake-like head with a serpentine tongue. It was crested and had scales befitting a dragon.

The name Mushussu's name was rendered in Akkadian but was based on an earlier Sumerian word. This word is sometimes interpreted to mean fierce snake, while some argue that the name should more properly be translated as the serpent of splendor. Some believe that this creature was not a mythical one representing the odd amalgamation of various parts of other animals, but that it actually represented a real creature that had once lived in the region. Some argue that the Mushussu was a stylized representation of an extinct giraffelike animal while others say that it is not stylized at all:

that the long-lost animal actually existed in the form depicted on the Ishtar Gate.

Nabu

Nabu was the patron divinity of writing and god of scribes. Nabu was worshipped by the Assyrians as well as the Babylonians. Nabu increased in prominence in the Babylonian period, especially around 1000 BC and later. This god was identified as the son of the important god Marduk, which dramatically increased his significance during this period. Nabu was a god of wisdom. He was said to be the inventor of that highly important innovation of the Mesopotamians: writing. Nabu was said, as the patron of writing, to write down the fates of all men. He was associated in this role with another god, Ninurta.

Nabu's iconography depicted him with a horn capped. As you have seen, horns were an important representation both of the gods and of power in Mesopotamia as this iconography frequently appears on gods, goddesses, and demons in this region. Nabu was depicted with his hands clasped, which was a gesture associated with priests, one of the more important feudal classes in Sumer. Nabu rode Sirrush, which was a dragon. Sirrush originally belonged to Nabu's father Marduk.

To the Babylonians, Nabu was associated with the planet Mercury. Like Inanna/Ishtar and some others, Nabu continued to be worshipped in Mesopotamia until very late.

Nergal

Nergal is an interesting god because of references made to him outside of Mesopotamian texts. Nergal was a god of the underworld. He was described in many myths as the consort of Ereshkigal, who was the ruler of the underworld and the sister of Inanna, the Queen of Heaven. Nergal's seat of worship was at the city of Cuthah, also known as Cuth. Nergal was worshipped very late in the period, with some of the most striking imagery of him coming from the Parthians. The Parthians ruled a large multi-ethnic empire from about 200 BC to about 200 AD. A Parthian relief shows Nergal as a bearded man with coiled hair, wearing Parthian-style attire, holding weapons in each hand, and holding dogs on a leash. On this relief, Nergal's consort Ereshkigal is shown in the background.

Nergal was mentioned in the Bible as the patron divinity of the city of Cuth, which is usually known today as Cuthah. The Babylonian equivalent of Nergal, according to the Bible, was Succoth-benoth. Talmudic scholars say that the name Nergal meant "dunghill rooster" and that the symbol of Nergal was the cockerel. Nergal is, however, usually associated with the lion as his emblem. Nergal was described as being the son of Ninlil and Enlil. His siblings were Ninurta and Nanna.

Ninhursag

Ninhursag was one of the seven great divinities of the Sumerians. She was a mother goddess of the mountains of Sumer, which is interesting as Sumer was not a mountainous region. Ninhursag had various other names, not unlike other gods of the Sumerians and Mesopotamians. Ninhursag was also known as Ninmah and Damgalnuna. She was mostly a goddess of fertility. Ninhursag seems to take on some of the roles of Inanna as she is called the Great Lady of heaven. It was said that the Sumerian kings were nourished by Ninhursag's milk.

Ninhursag's iconography shows her wearing a horned helmet. She wore a tiered skirt, which was often shown on goddesses of the region, like Inanna, for example. She carries weapons, indicating her status as a major divinity. She carries a mace and is occasionally accompanied by a lion. Ninhursag was associated with a symbol that resembled the Greek letter omega. The Egyptian goddess Hathor was also associated with such a symbol, and some have supposed that this symbol was really a stylized womb. Ninhursag's primary temple was at Eridu, although she also had a temple in the city of Kish.

Ninurta

Ninurta was the god of war in the Sumerian pantheon. He was also associated with scribes, farming, hunting, and justice.

Ninurta was a god of the earliest times. He was originally a god of agriculture who protected human beings from demonic forces. Ninurta took on a warrior role as Sumer's international position began to grow and war became more important. Indeed, a pattern of deities assuming a war role commensurate with the needs of the city-state or the people can be seen all over Mesopotamia as well as in other areas like Greece. Even Athena took on the role of the warrior as protector of her city of Athens.

Ninurta was also known as Ningirsu and he was the son of Ninhursag and Enlil, although, sometimes, he was described as the son of Ninlil and Enlil. Ninurta became an important divinity of the Assyrians because of the warrior attributes that he possessed at the time of the Assyrian Empire. Ninurta's chief center of worship had originally been at Nippur but became the city of Kalhu from the Assyrian period onward. Ninurta also had an important temple at Lagash that was rebuilt by King Gudea. Ninurta was often depicted as a wing warrior brandishing thunderbolt. He appeared in several myths, including the myth of Anzu's theft of the Tablet of Destinies.

Nanna

Nanna, also known as Sin, was a god of wisdom and the moon. Other names for this divinity include Suen. Nanna was the Sumerian name. Sin was a Semitic name that came to characterize some of the other societies that adopted this divinity after the Sumerian and Akkadian periods. Nanna was worshipped far and wide, as a divinity with the name Nanna was also worshipped in the southern reaches of the Arabian Peninsula.

Nanna was worshipped in many cities, but especially in the city of Ur. The Ziggurat of Ur was dedicated to Nanna indicating the importance of the worship of this divinity. Nanna was called by the name Lord of Wisdom or Enzu. As the roles of gods in Mesopotamia was constantly shifting, at one point, Nanna was regarded as the most important god in the pantheon. As Sin, Nanna was called the Creator of all Things and the Father of the Gods. These are names that are usually given to the heads of pantheons, such as Zeus and Odin, in the Greek and Norse pantheons, respectively. Nanna was married to Nergal, and they were the parents of Inanna and UtuShamash. In iconography, Nanna-Sin was shown sporting a beard of lapis lazuli. He was also shown riding a bull with wings.

Ninlil

Ninlil, or Mulliltu, is the consort of Enlil, at one time, the chief god of the Sumerians. Ninlil was called the Lady of the Wind. There were several important stories about Ninlil. She was impregnated by Enlil while she was lying by the river. She gave birth to her son Nanna afterward. As punishment, Enlil was sent down into the underworld where Ninlil joined him. There she gave birth to her son Nergal who became the consort of Ereshkigal, the Queen of the Underworld. She also gave birth in the underworld to Nunazau, who like Nergal, was described as a god of the underworld. She had a fourth son with her husband while he was disguised as a boatman; she gave birth to Enbilulu who was a god of waterways (canals and rivers).
Ninlil was also known as Sud.

Pazuzu

Pazuzu was a demonic god who protected human beings from evil forces and pestilence.

Sarpanit

Sarpanit was the name of the consort of the important Babylonian god Marduk.

Scorpion People

The Scorpion People were servants of the god Utu-Shamash.

Sin

Sin was an alternative name for Nanna, a moon god.

Tiamat

Tiamat was an important goddess of the early Sumerian pantheon. Tiamat was a goddess of the salt sea. She mated with the god of the freshwater sea, Abzu, to have children who became the younger gods and goddesses of Sumer. She was a god of anger who fought against the gods. She was regarded as the embodiment of the chaos of the primordial period. Although not described as a giant or giantess, Tiamat hearkens to the later myths of the Titans of Greece or the Giants (Jotun) of Norse myth.

Tiamat has an interesting double nature. She represents both the energy that drives creation, as she gives birth to important gods of the pantheon. But Tiamat also represents chaos and destruction, and in this guise, is sometimes identified as a dragon or serpent. Again, the myth of Tiamat and her husband
Abzu (or Apsu) resembles that of the Titans. After Tiamat gives birth to godly children, her husband fears that they will try to attack, overthrow, and kill him. Apsu is killed and Tiamat makes war against her children. She takes the form of a giant sea serpent. Tiamat is killed by Marduk, but before this, she gives birth to a few monsters. These monsters included dragons that had poison flowing in their veins rather than blood. This seems like an inspiration for the acid-filled veins of the Xenomorphs from Ridley Scott's Alien movies. Whether Tiamat should be described as a goddess or a dragoness is still up for debate.

Usmu

Usmu was a messenger god and the divinity of the city of Ea. He was the attendant of the important god Enki.

Utu-Shamash

Utu, or Shamash, was the god of the sun. This divinity was also associated with truth, morality, and justice. In this respect, Utu-Shamash seems to be similar to the Greek god Apollo who was also associated with justice, moderation, and morality in addition to being the god of the sun. This is an important connection as it has long been proposed that Apollo did not originate with the Greeks. Scholars believed that the original sun deity of the Greeks was most likely a female and that invaders brought a cadre of male gods including a male sun divinity.

Utu-Shamash was the twin brother of Inanna. This is easy to remember for those trying to learn connections between the Sumerian divinities because Apollo was the twin brother of Artemis. Although Artemis is distinct from Inanna, it could be said that the worship of Artemis in the Eastern regions of the Greek world like Ephesus in Ionia was not dissimilar to how Inanna was worshipped as Queen of Heaven. Utu-Shamash appeared in a number of important Sumerian myths. For example, he aided Gilgamesh in his battles against Humbaba, the ogre. Utu-Shamash was usually described as the offspring of Nanna and Ningal, but sometimes, he was said to be the son of Anu or Enlil. The main cities devoted to Utu-Shamash were at Sippar and Larsa.

Chapter 3: Tales of Gods and Goddesses

All mythologies are made up of the tales that were told about the gods, goddesses, and heroes of the society. In some cases, the tales of these characters were told orally, while in other cases, they were inscribed. Sumer was interesting because, although it was such an early society, many of the epics, poems, and stories were inscribed on cuneiform, which has allowed these stories to be transmitted to us in the present. In this chapter, we will have a formal introduction to Sumerian myth by examining several important tales of the gods and goddesses of Sumer. These include the Sumerian creation myth, which centered around a series of so-called cosmic births.

The Cosmic Births

The Sumerians believed the universe to be a dome surrounded by a sea of saltwater. Both the earth and the underworld were a part of this construct, with a freshwater sea called the Apsu also being located here. The main deities of this early universe were An and Ki. An was the god of the heavens while Ki was the ruler of the underworld. Over time, the concept of the underworld evolved into a place called Kur that was ruled by the goddess Ereshkigal. In a poem about Gilgamesh, Enkidu, and the Underworld, the tale of the Cosmic Births - the beginning of life - is told.

First, there was only Nammu, which is the name given to the sea from the earliest recesses of time. It was the existence of this primeval sea that would begin the process of Cosmic Births. Water was important symbolically to the Mesopotamians as the water was necessary for civilization to take route. Water allowed for large scale agriculture rather than mere hunting, gathering, and fishing for food. Freshwater also permitted the rise of large-scale settlements called cities, which formed the basis of the civic life that characterized the first civilizations.

From Nammu, the primordial sea was born An and Ki, the first births. An was the god of the sky (or the heavens) and Ki was the earth. An mated with Ki to produce additional births. The first birth to Ki was Enlil who was the god of storm, wind, and rain. It would be Enlil that would formally separate heaven from the earth. Enlil took the earth as his domain while An, or Anu, was able to retain control of the sky.

One final note about the heavens. The Sumerians saw the heavens as consisting of several domes. There were typically three in myths and poems, but, sometimes, there were as many as seven. These domes existed over the earth, which was perceived to be flat. The lowest of the three domes were made of jasper stone and it was the abode of the starry sky. The second dome was made of a stone called Saggilmut, and this was the home of the Igigi. The highest of the three domes were made of a stone called luludanitu and An was the embodiment of this.

The other major celestial bodies were Venus, which was embodied by Inanna. The sun was Inanna's brother Utu (or Shamash). The moon was Nanna, who was the father to both Utu and Inanna. Human beings did not go to heaven as this was the abode of the gods alone. Instead, humans went down to Kur, or Irkalla, when they died: an underworld filled with shadows.

Enki and the Creation of Life

Cosmology was highly important to the Sumerians. They were talented astrologists and their observations and naming of the stars contributed to the knowledge that existed in other nearby civilizations like the Greeks and the Egyptians. The Cosmic Birth myth was not the only story that was closely tied to the cosmological principles that the Sumerians believed in. An important concept among the Sumerians was hieros gamos.

Hieros gamos is actually a Greek word that refers to a sacred marriage. This was a marriage in which opposite principles of male and female were combined to give birth to cosmic life. This belief is another example of a Sumerian cosmic principle, but it also underlies the union of An and Ki to give birth to Enlil and subsequently life. The tale of Enki and Ninhursag, which will be related shortly, explains how Enki is living with his wife in Dimun, which is a paradise. Enki is lord of Ab, which means freshwater, but which can also refer to male semen.

The idea of the sacred marriage actually exists in other cultures outside of Mesopotamia. In Hinduism, there was a ritual where girls were dedicated to a temple, which was perceived as a sort of marriage to the god that involved dance and other rituals. For the Greeks, the marriage of Zeus and Hera was the most important sacred marriage, and this would have been reenacted at ceremonies, especially on the island of Samos where the marriage was said to take place. In Sumer, it was important that the kings undertake a sacred marriage to the priestess of Inanna, representing the union from which the life and welfare of the people in the city-state would spring.

In a poem, much detail is given about the land of Dimun that Enki travels to. Dimun was described as a place that was clean and pure. It was also bright. Dimun almost resembles the garden of Eden is much attention is paid to the fact that, in Dimun, lions, wolves, dogs, and other wild animals did not kill or snatch. Boar did not devour grain either.

Enlil and Ninlil

Ninlil was the goddess consort of Enlil. We have already been exposed to Enlil, who, at times, was the chief god of the Sumerians. Enlil was the child born to An and Ki, the heaven and the earth, and he replaced his mother as ruler of the earth.

In addition, Enlil was responsible for wind, air, and storms. Enlil is also known as Ellil or Elil, and Nunamnir. The story of Enlil and Ninlil is encapsulated in a 152-line poem of Sumer. It describes the relationship of Enlil and Ninlil.

The poem begins with the city where the story takes place. The tale begins in the city of Nippur, which was also called DurJicnimbar. This city was washed in the waters of the River IdSala, a holy river. Kar-Jectina is the name of one of its quays while Kar-Asar is another quay where swift ships are made. The holy canal of Nippur was called Id-Numbir-Tum. It is a grand canal that branches yielding much-cultivated land

The poem continues and Ninlil is instructed to bathe in the river by her mother Nunbarsheganu though she is warned about the potential advances of Enlil should she stray near the river. Enlil finds Ninlil naked at the riverside and impregnates her. There is born to them a first son, Nanna, god of the moon.

In consequence, Enlil is banished to Kur: the underworld. Ninlil, curious to know where Enlil has gone, follows him. At this point, Enlil is impersonating the gatekeeper of the underworld and impregnates Ninlikl with a second child, Nergal. As related earlier, Ninlil is seduced a third time and gives birth to the god Nunazu. The last child born as a result of Enlil's seductions is Enbilulu, a god who is sometimes described as the inspector of canals.

The poem of Enlil and Ninlil draws to a close with a singing of the praises of the twain. Enlil, who is called by different names, is praised as king, lord, supreme lord, and other grand titles. He is the Lord who makes the produce of Sumer grow, and he is also lord of the earth as well as heaven. He is the Lord who makes judgments that cannot be broken, and the lord whose spoken words cannot be altered. Ninlil is also praised as a mother right alongside Father Enlil as he is called.

The Atra-Hasis

Atrahasis, or the Epic of Atrahasis, is the most complete account of the Great Flood in Mesopotamian literature. The tale was adapted as a part of the Epic of Gilgamesh though some of the characters' names were altered. The Atrahasis (also Atra-Hasis) was written during the Akkadian period. Recall that the Akkadians were the people dwelling to the immediate north of the Sumerians proper. During the Akkadian period, which began with King Sargon, the Akkadians and Sumerians were unified into a single state known as the Akkadian Empire.

The Epic of Atrahasis was written around 1800 BC. It was recorded in the Semitic Akkadian language upon clay tablets. The name indicated that the contents of the tablets contained great wisdom. The contents included a Sumerian creation story as well as the story of the Great Flood. Atrahasis was not only the name for this work. The name also appears on the Sumerian King List, meaning that it indicates a king of a Sumerian city-state; in this case, the city of Shuruppak. This king lived in antediluvian times.

The Atrahasis begins with events antecedent to the Deluge. Before the Great Flood or the Deluge, the Seven Great Gods of Sumer were abusing the lesser Igigi gods with labor, according to the text of the Atrahasis. The Seven Great Gods of Sumer were Enlil, An, Enki, Utu, Inanna, Ninhursag, and Nanna. Although sometimes, used as a synonymous term with Annunaki, Igigi in the Epic of Atrahasis referred to the lesser gods who were servants to the Seven Great Gods.

The Igigi, or lesser divinities, rebelled about 40 years after they had been tasked with farm work by Enlil. Rather than punish the Igigi, Enki decided to trick humans into doing the work instead. A goddess called Mami is tasked with creating humans, which she does by shaping figurines out of clay mixed with blood and flesh. Lastly, the gods spit upon the clay. Ten months later, a womb that was specially made splits and the humans come to life. Following this creation, the human population deals with overpopulation. Enlil, who is depicted as being cruel, sends a pestilence every 1200 years to reduce the population. Enlil eventually decides to destroy humans with a flood. Enki knows of this plan but is sworn to secrecy.

The third tablet of the Atrahasis contains the flood myth. This would be the tablet that would be adapted into the deluge story in the Epic of Gilgamesh. Enki tells a hero called Atrahasis about Enlil's plan. He instructs Atrahasis to dismantle his house and build a large boat that is tightly sealed with bitumen. When the time is right, Atrahasis boards the ship he has made with his wife, children, and animals. A storm comes that is so intense that even the gods and goddesses of Sumer are frightened. The flood ends after seven days. Atrahasis sacrifices to the gods while Enlil becomes enraged with Enki for thwarting his plans to control the human population.

Enki and Ninhursag

This is the tale of how water can bring life to arid lands. Historians of myth believe it to be related to other myths and tales about the forbidden fruit, such as the tale of Adam and Eve in the Garden of Eden. As we have seen, Enki was a god who was often associated with rivers and riverbanks. After Enki impregnated Ninhursag, she was with child for nine days and then gave birth to Ninsar. Enki later comes upon Ninsar and, not knowing her to be his daughter, he impregnates her as well. She gives birth to a daughter called Ninkurra. Enki is left alone and eventually comes upon Ninkurra. He sires a child with her, too, and this child is Uttu (not to be confused with Utu).

Enki comes upon Uttu and tries to sire a child with her as well. Uttu's name meant spider. Uttu was familiar with Enki's reputation for seduction and goes to Ninhursag for advice. Ninhursag advises her to avoid riversides, which is an area that Enki tends to frequent. In a different version of this story, Ninhursag takes the semen that Enki fertilized in Uttu's womb and uses it to plant eight rapidly growing plants. But Enki cannot seem to give up his old ways. He eats the eight fruits, which causes him to become pregnant. He experiences great pain as he does not have a birth canal to give birth through. A fox advises Enki to turn to Ninhursag, the woman he initially seduced, for aid. She offers to take the offspring into her own womb and gives birth to gods of healing: Abu, Nintul, Ninsutu, Ninkasi, Daziuma, Ninti, and Eshagag.

Chapter 4: The Exploits of Ninurta

Ninurta was an important god of Mesopotamian myth. Ninurta was a god of thunder and rainstorms. He was also the god of spring. Ninurta was associated with plowing, floods, and agriculture in general. He received particular devotion from farmers. His name in cuneiform may be read as Anzu, and in early iconography, he appeared as an enormous bird. He became more humanized over time, but the symbolism of lions, birds, and other animals was still associated with him.

Ninurta was depicted as a warrior who used a bow and arrow as well as a mace. He rides a lion with a scorpion tail in some images. He was the son of Enlil and Ninlil, although, on occasion, other mothers are ascribed to him. He was married to Gula. One of the more important stories of Ninurta was that of the theft of the Tablet of Destinies by the Anzu bird. The tablets held the fate of god and mortal. The tablets could legitimize a man who wished to be king. Ninurta offers to help Enlil get the tablets back. Ninurta launches arrows at the Anzu bird, but the creature uses the Tablet of Destinies to reverse time, sending the arrows back to the states they were originally: wood, feathers, et cetera. Ninurta eventually is able to tear off the bird's wings and return the tablets to Enlil.

Ninurta was a particularly important god to the Assyrians. They built massive statues of him and made many dedications to the god. Some even included Ninurta in their names. When the Assyrian Empire declined and fell (several times in fact), the image of Ninurta suffered greatly. Because he was so honored by the kings, his failure to protect them caused the people to question his power. The tale of Ninurta and the Tablet of Destinies is not the only important story in which Ninurta was a primary character. Here we will learn other tales of this important here from Sumerian myth.

Ninurta and Asag (including Ninurta and Ninmah)

One of the themes of the tale of Ninurta and the Tablet of Destinies is that Ninurta was brave. He was the only Sumerian divinity who was willing to battle the Anzu bird to bring the tablet back to Enlil, who was the chief of all the gods. At one time, Ninurta is encouraged to travel to the underworld to face Agag or Asag. Ninurta falls for this trickery (which some say came from his mace) and soon learns that Asag was a force to be reckoned with. Asag was assisted by rock monsters and plant animals forming quite a challenge for Ninurta.

Ninurta attempts to flee, but his mace reminds him of his bravery and all the great feats he has already accomplished. Ninurta turns around and defeats the warriors assisting Asag as well as Asag himself. The death of Asag meant that the waters below the earth would rise out of the underworld and prevent farmers from growing crops. Ninurta constructs a wall that eventually forms a mountain that traps a mountain. Ninurta is congratulated by his mother, Ninmah, who is subsequently given a new name after the mountain: Ninhursag.

Ninurta and the Turtle

Ninurta was credited with possessing spells that could ward off disease, demons, and other ill things. Enki compliments Ninurta on what he has done so far, but this only makes Ninurta angry as he feels it is not quite enough for him. Enki creates an enormous turtle which then turns on Ninurta. It begins to chew on the ankles of the god. They engage in battle, which results in the formation of a large pit that has been partially dug by the turtle. They fall into this pit. Enki looks down at Ninurta in the pit and scoffs at him. He is amused that the god is being gnawed on by the turtle. The story was intended to humble Ninurta a bit in his pride.

Ninurta's Return to Nippur

The tale of Ninurta and Asag, in which Ninurta's mace Sharur encourages him to go to the underworld, appears in a work called the Lugal-E. A companion to this work is the so-called Angim Dimma, which tells of Ninurta's Return to Nippur after defeating Asag. This tale praises Ninurta, comparing him favorably to the god Anu (or An). The tale starts with the desire for Ninurta to visit his father Enlil at his court in Nippur. He comes to visit his father and mother dressed splendidly in royal attire. A messenger comes to Ninurta to tell him that his dress is so magnificent that it would be wise to tone it down a bit in order to pay respects to his father. Ninurta lays aside some of his weapons, though not all of them, and then enters the temple of Enlil. Here he is happily welcomed by the other gods of the Anunnaki.

Chapter 5: Tales of Kings and Heroes

There was a fine line between the heroic king and the true hero in Sumerian myth. The king was an idealized figure around whom a story of some great accomplishment was erected. The poems that were written in Sumerian times praise these heroes and kings with a formula that is quite distinct. Repetition is used to emphasize the great qualities of these characters. They are praised for their wisdom, their strength, their loyalty, and a host of other traits that must have been perceived as necessary to the country (or city-state) or worth encouraging in the population: those people who would hear these tales.

Enmerkar and the Lord of Aratta

Enmerkar was a king of Uruk, which is known as Unug or Kulaba in the series of four tales that deal with his exploits. Some of these tales are covered in this chapter while others are mentioned later. Enmerkar was involved in contests with the lord of the king of the city of Aratta. These battles involve the lord of Aratta attempting to conquer Uruk and occasionally Enmerkar attempting to conquer the city of Aratta. Enmerkar was an important figure. He was said to have founded the city of Uruk and to have built a large temple at Eridu. Enmerkar had an association with language and writing that is often mentioned in ancient sources.

It is this latter subject that is mentioned in the present tale. The tale of Enmerkar and the Lord of Aratta involves the socalled confusion of the tongues in the world. As the reader will learn, versions of some Sumerian stories appear to be very similar to stories which later appeared in the Bible. The tale begins with a description of Uruk and the relationship between Enmerkar and Inanna, who is called the queen of all the lands. Enmerkar crowns himself in the name of Inanna, but she is not particularly pleased with this. Enmerkar asks for the goddess's help in subduing Aratta, and she suggests sending an envoy to the ruler there to demand submission.

Enmerkar sends the envoy to the king of Aratta. The ruler says that he cannot submit to Enmerkar because it was Inanna and Inanna alone who chose him for the office he now occupies. But the king is devastated when he learns that Enmerkar built a temple to Inanna and that the goddess was the one who promised to help submit Aratta. The king agrees to submit if Enmerkar will send him a large supply of barley and provide proof that Inanna supports Uruk rather than Aratta.

Enmerkar sends the requested grain as well as the promise to send some precious stones.

The king of Aratta becomes infuriated and only agrees to accept the stones if Enmerkar brings them himself. Enmerkar spends the next 10 years creating a rich jeweled scepter which he sends to Aratta with a messenger. The king of Uruk wants to engage in one-on-one combat to prove which king is the greater. Messages go back and forth between the two kings, which confuses Enmerkar's messenger who cannot remember them all. Enmerkar thus invents writing on tablets to solve this problem that has arisen. The tale ends with Enmerkar triumphant and the people of Aratta sending tribute to the temple of Inanna in Uruk.

Enmerkar and the Ensuhkesdanna

Enmerkar and the Ensuhkesdanna is essentially a follow-up to the story of Enmerkar and the Lord of Aratta. It is one of a number of tales that deal with the contest between Enmerkar and the city of Aratta. This tale is also known as Enmerkar and the En-suhgir-ana. Other tales regarding the lord of Aratta do not give his name, but in this particular tale, this ruler is known as Ensuhkesdanna or En-suhgir-ana. As in other tales on this subject, Enmerkar is the king of Uruk (called Unug of Kulaba in the tale), which is described as reaching from the heavens to the earth.

The tale begins with Ensuhkesdanna demanding that Enmerkar submits to him. He also brags that he has closer ties to the goddess Inanna than Enmerkar has. The envoy delivers this message to Enmerkar who replies that Inanna would not deign to spend a short time with Ensuhkesdanna. On the other hand, Enmerkar enjoys her company quite a bit (and the tale delves into some interesting descriptions about the dalliances between Enmerkar and Inanna, including how loudly the goddess yells when she is enjoying Enmerkar's private attention; if you know what we mean). Receiving this message, Ensuhkesdanna feels forlorn, but he vows never to give up in his contest against Enmerkar.

A sorcerer called Urgirinuna appears at this point and he says that he can make Enmerkar submit. The chief minister agrees to the sorcerer's plan to disrupt the important livestock that Enmerkar keeps at the city of Eresh. But Urgirinuna's machinations with the livestock were observed, which leads a sorceress to appear to challenge him. They engage in a series of contests that involves the sorceress besting the animals that Urgirinuna conjures with predators. The sorceress triumphs over the sorcerer of Aratta and tosses him into the River Euphrates. Ensuhkesdanna subsequently admits defeat.

Sargon and Ur-Zababa

Sargon was the founder of the Akkadian Empire. A review of his life will be detailed extensively in a later chapter dealing with Akkadian religion and civilization. Sargon, before he became a great king and founder of an empire, was cupbearer to the ruler of Kish. That ruler was King Ur-Zababa. A cupbearer was a high honor in ancient times as it provided the person who held the role with close access to the sovereign. Recall that both Ganymede and Hebe in Greek myth held the position of cupbearer to the gods of Mount Olympus, even then clearly a place of high honor.

The story of Sargon and Ur-Zababa is told in a tale known as the Sargon Legend. This text is taken to be the biography of Sargon's life. In the text, Ur-Zababa appoints Sargon as his cupbearer after awakening from a dream. Ur-Zababa subsequently invites Sargon to his bedchamber to discuss a dream that Sargon had. This dream involved the favor that Inanna planned to bestow upon Sargon. Ur-Zababa is left frightened by the message of this dream. Subsequently, UrZababa sends Sargon to the king of Uruk, King Lugal-zage-sir, bearing a tablet instructing the king to kill Sargon.

Chapter 6: Tales of Inanna

Inanna was the Sumerian divinity who appeared in more myths and tales than any other. She was a frequently mentioned character in the significant Epic of Gilgamesh, and she was mentioned in most of the stories that involved heroes like Lugalbanda and Enmerkar, and villains like the Lord of Aratta. Inanna was a deity whose cult increased in prominence over time. She seemed to possess an irresistible power that drew kings and peoples to her.

In tales involving Enmerkar and the Lord of Aratta (an interaction that was part of a four-story cycle), Inanna is often invoked in a lascivious matter. This is interesting because it suggests that the Sumerian people did not find references of female deities involved in sex with common people offensive, something which probably would not have gone over so well with the Greeks and Romans. As Inanna is mentioned so frequently in this book, in this chapter, we will focus on two stories involving this important goddess who was also known as Istarte, Astarte, Ishtar, and Ashtoreth. These are the tales of Inanna and Ebih and Inanna and the Huluppu Tree.

Inanna and Ebih

Inanna and her brother, the sun god Utu, were important arbiters of justice in the Sumerian world. Several myths that include Inanna show her in this role and the tale of Inanna and Ebih is one of those. This tale is also known as Goddess of the Fearsome Divine Powers. It is a poem nearly two hundred lines long, and it was written by the poet Enheduanna who was writing in the Akkadian period. As with many tales of this type (that is, epic poems), this particular tale begins by singing the praises of Inanna. It was common for such tales to praise a god or place at the beginning of the work.

After Inanna is praised, the work describes the travels of Inanna around the world. During her travels, she comes across a mountain know as Mount Ebih. This mountain is lofty and beautiful; Inanna considers its existence offensive to her own dignity. I suppose we might describe Inanna as having Narcissistic Personality Disorder today. All jokes aside, Inanna launches into a soliloquy where she explains why she is angry at the mountain and desires to destroy it. She mentions that it is lofty, beautiful, does press its mouth humbly into the dust, and other things. Inanna asks An to allow her to destroy Mount Ebih. Inanna ignores An's urging to leave the mountain be and attacks it anyway. She destroys the mountain and subsequently explains again why she attacked it.

Inanna and the Huluppu Tree

The tale of Inanna and the Huluppu Tree is found in a wellknown poem called Gilgamesh, Enkidu, and the Netherworld. This poem has been mentioned elsewhere in this work. It is a distinct work from the Epic of Gilgamesh, which was written hundreds of years after the original Gilgamesh poems were compiled. In this work, Inanna is yet young and even headier than she will later be. The story begins with a tree called the Huluppu tree. Some scholars have identified this tree with the weeping willow. This tree is growing on the banks of the Euphrates River, and Inanna wants to move it to her garden in order to shape it into a throne once it is done growing.

The tree grows in Inanna's garden in Uruk, just as she wants it to, but eventually, it becomes home to a number of unsavory creatures; namely, an Anzu bird, a charmless serpent, and a creature called Lilitu in Sumerian. On a side note, Lilitu is the antecedent to the character of Lilith who will appear later in Jewish texts. Gilgamesh comes along and slays the serpent that is lacking in charms. In this tale, Gilgamesh is described as the brother of Inanna. After the charmless serpent is slain, the Lilitu and the Anzu bird flee. Gilgamesh's mates cut down the huluppu tree and use its wood to make the throne that Inanna wanted. They subsequently give the throne to Inanna.

Inanna herself makes two objects called a mikku and a pikku, which she gifts to the hero as a reward for his efforts to help her.

Chapter 7: Tales of Nanna

Nanna was the god of the moon in Sumerian mythology, and as such, there were a number of important myths and stories told about him. As we have seen, Nanna was also known as Sin or Suen. In actuality, Nanna and Sin were originally two separate deities. Nanna was the Sumerian deity. In fact, the cuneiform name of the important city of Ur was literally "the abode of Nanna." Nanna was a very old deity whose importance was closely associated with the city of Ur. Indeed, some propose that Nanna was regarded as the chief deity of the pantheon in the Sumerian religion during the supremacy of Ur (around 2600 BC).

Sin was originally a Semitic deity. Recall that Sumerian was not a Semitic language and the infiltration of Semitic languages into Mesopotamia was associated with the Akkadian period and afterward. During the Akkadian period, the Semitic god Sin or Suen came to be associated with Nanna. There was particular iconography associated with this god, including the crescent moon and the bull, although the bull was associated with other divinities as well. The name Suen is especially associated with the Assyrian period and it refers to a lamp or source of illumination that became associated with the moon god as early as the Akkadian period. Another name of this god is En-Zu, which is occasionally written in Assyrian as the number 30.

Priests were very important in Sumer as well as Mesopotamia as a whole. Priests of the chief god were able to wield great power. During the reign of the Babylonian king Nabonidus, who reigned from 556 BC to 539 BC, appointed his mother as the high priestess of Nanna in the city of Harran, while his daughter was appointed high priestess in the city of Ur. Historians say that this act allowed King Nabonidus to consolidate his power both politically and religiously, much like Sargon was able to to do in the Akkadian Empire nearly 2000 years before. Sargon had also made his daughter priestess of Nanna at Ur. It is important to note that although Sargon is attested as early as 3500 BC, Sargon was one of his main promoters during his reign about one thousand years later.

The Journey of Nanna to Nippur

As with many other poems and tales in Sumerian myth, this particular tale begins with the singing of the praises of the city of Nippur. Later, Nanna loads his boat with all the great products of Ur, which he plans to display to his father at

Nippur. This is another tale in which the gods are presented as if engaging in the sorts of things as ordinary people do, not to mention having the same sorts of concerns.

Some of the things that Nanna loads are animals, plants, and trees. He sails upriver with these things, stopping at five cities along the way. He is greeted at each city and does do honor to each city's god. When he finally reaches Nippur, he is greeted by the gatekeeper who welcomes him royally. Nanna is brought into the presence of his father Enlil. He has a feast with his father and then proceeds to make a number of requests of Enlil. He asks for the fields to bloom with great harvest, for the river to become swollen with sweetly smelling water, for good luck in making wine and honey, and for longevity to partake of all these gifts. The god Enlil agrees to grant these requests and Nanna subsequently returns to Ur.

Other Tales of Nanna

Nanna had a number of other roles besides his association with the moon and fertility. The Babylonians believed that Nanna was the offspring of Marduk, their chief god. It was Marduk who placed Nanna (the moon) in the sky. The Babylonians believed that lunar eclipses resulted from demons attempting to steal the moonlight, and Nanna had to be diligent in fighting them in order to allow the moon to continue to shine down upon the earth.

In one tale, Nanna is described as standing in judgment of the dead. This is a role that Nanna acquired a little later in his worship. The Queen of the Dead was Ereshkigal, the sister of Inanna, but Ereshkigal was not generally believed to pass judgment over those that had died and come to her realm. Hers was a dark, shadowy place. In one particular inscription, Nanna is said to judge the dead in the underworld (or netherworld) and to help them obtain food and drink (beer) there. This may represent a further exploration of daily life in the netherworld, or it may embody an expanding role for Nanna as one of the more important gods in the Sumerian pantheon.

Chapter 8: The Epic of Gilgamesh

The Epic of Gilgamesh was a poem written circa 1800 BC. It is known as an epic poem because it tells the tale of a hero and is written in a poetic pattern. The story was written in Akkadian, which, at this time, was one of the major languages of Sumer (it had already begun to replace the Sumerian language in this part of Mesopotamia). The Epic of Gilgamesh is the story of how Gilgamesh comes to the aid of the goddess Inanna but later angers her. Inanna gives Gilgamesh a pair of objects, which he misplaces. In this tale, Gilgamesh learns from Enkidu of the conditions in the underworld of Kur. Gilgamesh also overthrows his suzerain, King Agga. Other poems in this epic tell how Gilgamesh defeats Huwawa, an ogre. A final epic poem tells of Gilgamesh's death and burial.

Gilgamesh was a king of the city of Uruk, which was one of the most important city-states in Sumer. Gilgamesh was the hero of the Epic of Gilgamesh, which was actually a series of poems. These poems were written at different dates, and some poems are in a better state of preservation than others. It is believed that the earliest of these poems was Gilgamesh, Enkidu, and the Netherworld. This is the poem where

Gilgamesh sends scurrying the creatures surrounding Inanna's huluppu tree.

After the death of Enkidu, Gilgamesh learns of the conditions in the "Netherworld."

The Epic of Gilgamesh was composed of separate poems about the life of Gilgamesh. The formal epic was written by a scribe called Sin-leqi-unninni around 1600 BC, but it was based on the epic poems that had been written earlier. Gilgamesh of the epic was a demigod who has dealings with Inanna (known at the time the epic was written as Ishtar). The real Gilgamesh was a king who lived sometime between 2900 BC and 2300 BC. This would place him just before the foundation of the Akkadian Empire by King Sargon. Although there are no remains from Gilgamesh's reign, a monument from the reign of King Ishbi-Erra of Sumer credits Gilgamesh with erecting the walls of the city of Uruk. Ishbi-Erra reigned as king circa 1900 BC.

Gilgamesh and Huwawa

Like many other Sumerian myths, the Epic of Gilgamesh begins by praising the city where the story takes place. The epic takes place in the city of Uruk, which according to the epic, is notable for its great buildings and the quality of its brickwork. Gilgamesh is the king in Uruk and a demigod. the people are displeased at how Gilgamesh is governing, as he is forcing them to labor hard, and they pray for the gods to send them someone to aid them. The gods send Enkidu who lives in the woods rather than in the city of Uruk with Gilgamesh and the other town dwellers. Enkidu learns about Gilgamesh from a hierodule, and he goes to the city of Uruk to challenge Gilgamesh to a match.

Gilgamesh wins the match, and Enkidu and Gilgamesh become fast friends. The twain set their sights on fighting Huwawa, who is a demon inhabiting the cedar forest. Cedar was highly valued at this time, and the east coast of the Mediterranean was famed for its cedars. Huwawa, also called Humbaba, is described as a giant who was raised by the sun, Utu. Huwawa was the guardian of this particular cedar forest, which was the abode of the gods. Huwawa had been assigned to this task by the Enlil, and he was said to be the terror of mortals.

Gilgamesh is the one who wants to go to Huwawa in order to establish his fame as he cannot live forever. Gilgamesh cajoles Huwawa into giving away his power by promising him his sisters as consorts for the giant. The giant's guard is now down and he is easily captured by Gilgamesh. The giant appeals for clemency, but Enkidu convinces his friend to slay him. The giant's head is placed in a sack, which is given to Enlil. Enlil becomes enraged, but he does not punish the hero.

Gilgamesh and Aga

Gilgamesh was living in Uruk when Aga (or Agga), the King of Kish, sent envoys to him. Gilgamesh summoned the elders and told them that they should not submit to Aga because there was work still to be done in Uruk. For example, the wells needed to be finished. Gilgamesh's suggestion was that they should smite Aga, the son of Enmebaragesi, with weapons. The elders believed that because there was work to be completed in Uruk, they should submit to Aga.

Gilgamesh decided not to take the advice of the elders. He was under the protection of Inanna, so he went to the strong men of the city and urged them to use weapons to fight back against Aga. The strong men of the city said that as Gilgamesh had built the walls of Uruk, and as he was a strong man and a warrior, that he should fight back. They believed that Aga would be sent fleeing with terror should Gilgamesh do so. Gilgamesh told his friend Enkidu to ready their weapons to prepare for battle.

Aga laid siege to Uruk soon afterward. During the siege, Aga and Gilgamesh exchange words. The warriors acknowledge Gilgamesh as king of Uruk. Gilgamesh sends his former overlord back to Kish but acknowledges the kindness that Aga has paid to him in the past. Aga returns to Kish and the praises of Gilgamesh are sung.

Gilgamesh and Utnapishtum

Ishtar propositions Gilgamesh, but he rejects her. He simply was not interested. Ishtar goes to her father, An, and obtains the Bull of Heaven to send against Gilgamesh. Gilgamesh and Enkidu smite the Bull of Heaven. The gods punish Enkidu by striking him with a fatal illness. Enkidu laments that he left his safe forest to come to the city of Uruk and Gilgamesh, but the hero reminds him of their friendship. Enkidu is glad that he met Gilgamesh and formed a friendship with him. Enkidu dies and Gilgamesh laments his passing.

At this point, Gilgamesh meets many different people who give him words of wisdom. Gilgamesh seeks out Utnapishtum, his ancestor, who lives at the rivers' mouth. Utnapishtum tells Gilgamesh that he survived the floodwaters because the god Ea warned him with enough advance warning so that he could dismantle his home and build an ark. The gods subsequently gave Utnapishtum immortal life. Gilgamesh believes that he should also be awarded immortal life. Utnapishtum tries to test Gilgamesh by bidding him to remain awake for a week's time, but Gilgamesh fails in this task. Utnapishtum tells Gilgamesh about a plant that can give him youth. Gilgamesh fetches the plant from its location in Dilmun (modern-day Bahrain), but the plant of youth is stolen by a serpent.

Gilgamesh returns to the city of Uruk where he has abandoned his dreams of eternal youth.

Enkidu in the Underworld

Enkidu has a terrible vision of the underworld. In this noncanonical poem of the epic, Enkidu sees the underworld as it truly is. The vision that Enkidu sees is gloomy. He curses Shamhat for civilizing him. Enkidu had begun the tale as a socalled wild man living outside of civilized places like Uruk. Enkidu later retracts the curse he laid on Shamhat after he is scolded by Utu. It was Shamhat who brought Enkidu into the pleasures that civilization represents. Enkidu is subsequently struck with illness by Inanna and later dies, to be mourned by Gilgamesh.

Chapter 9: Lighter Tales of Sumerian Gods and Heroes

Sumerian heroes were interesting because many of them, like Gilgamesh and Atrahasis, were real people who lived as kings before they entered the realm of myth. In the Epic of Gilgamesh, especially the formal epic that was written hundreds of years after the original epic poems (which formed the source material), Gilgamesh is described as half man and half god. This makes Gilgamesh essentially a demigod on the order of many of the heroes of the Greeks.

It is interesting to examine the position of the demigod in Sumerian myth as sort of a precursor to two specific tales about Sumerian heroes, namely tales involving the hero Lugulbanda. A demigod is literally someone who is not quite a god, but more than man. Although the place of the demigod in the canonical mythology of Sumer is similar to the place of the demigod among the Greeks, the latter was the demigod as a character with a specific identity. For them, the demigod was the son of a god or goddess by a mortal. Where the Greeks saw the godly lineage as being important, the Sumerians saw the great men as being inducted into semi-godly status by virtue of their great deeds. The result is not altogether different. Certainly, great kings and dynasties of Greek lands must have claimed a god for an ancestor as a way of legitimating their role. So where the Sumerians were practical about the matter - merely placing their great men as equal in stature to the gods - it would seem the Greeks doctored history somewhat and claimed that their great rulers were actually the sons of gods and thus true demigods, and not just exceptional mortals.

Lugalbanda in the Mountain Cave

Lugalbanda is a prime example of the Sumerian demigod. Although he is described as a real person, namely, the second king of the city of Uruk, he was said to have reigned for 1200 years, which is not exactly consistent with mortals. In this respect, this Sumerian ruler echoes the sorts of tales told about Egyptian pharaohs, many of whom were reputed to have lived well over one hundred years of age. It has been difficult to determine if Lugalbanda truly was a living person, although the evidence suggests that the Sumerians perceived him as being real. He was listed on their king lists after all.

Lugalbanda in the Mountain Cave is a story that is also known as Lugalbanda in the Wilderness. This story and others about Lugalbanda belong to a particular cycle of myths that are about conflicts between a king named Enmerkar and another king who ruled the city of Aratta. The story is quite old, from about 2100 BC, although the tablets that remain today are from about three hundred years later.

The story begins with Enmerkar marching on the city of Aratta at the head of a large army. One of his soldiers is Lugalbanda. Unfortunately for the warrior, he falls ill and his brothers leave him in a cave. It will be up to the gods whether he survives this desertion or dies. Lugalbanda prays to several gods, namely, Inanna, Shamash, and Nanna. He prays to be healed of the illness that has struck him down. The gods answer his prayer and eventually, Lugalbanda is able to leave the cave. He hunts a bull and two wild goats before laying down to dream. Lugalbanda has a dream where he is told to offer the animals to the gods in sacrifice. Lugalbanda awakens and does as the dream has instructed him. Although the rest of the tale has been obscured by the passage of thousands of years, it seems to reflect the dual nature of the gods as both munificent and sometimes cruel.

Lugalbanda and the Anzu Bird

Lugalbanda and the Anzu bird is a story that follows Lugalband in the Wilderness (or Lugalbanda in the Mountain Cave) in sequence. This tale also is part of the cycle of stories that involve Enmerkar in his battles against a king (whose name has been lost) of Aratta. Like the previous tale, this one was written about 2100 BC with the remaining records of it dating to about 1800 BC.

The tale of Lugalbanda and the Anzu birds begin with the hero traveling through the highlands. He stumbles across the hatched chick of the Anzu bird. We have encountered this creature before, but it is essentially a giant eagle with the head of a lion. Lugalbanda feeds the chick while its parent is away. When the Anzu bird returns, it is startled that the chick does not heed its call. But it learns that Lugalbanda has been tending the chick and decides to reward the hero. The Anzu bird gives Lugalbanda the ability to travel great distances in a short period of time. Sort of like Superman's ability to "leap tall buildings at a single bound," et cetera.

With his new ability in tow, Lugalbanda returns to his king Enmerkar who is still laying siege to Aratta but having great difficulty in this endeavor. Enmerkar desires to go to Inanna to plead with her for aid in the siege. Lugalbanda offers to make the trip, which he is able to do swiftly because of the ability he has been granted by the Anzu bird. When he reaches Inanna, Lugalbanda is given instructions on how the army can overcome the powerful city of Aratta.

Chapter 10: The Akkadian Empire and Mythology

The first empire of Mesopotamia was that of the Akkadians. Their state is dated from approximately 2334 BC to 2194 BC. The Akkadian Empire included Sumer proper as well as areas to the north. It encompassed most of modern-day Iraq; it also included parts of Turkey, Syria, and Kuwait. Akkad was important not only as the first empire that is known to us, but also in terms of the art, architecture, religion, and advancements that are exported to other regions. In this chapter, we will solidify our understanding of Sumerian society and religion by examining what some might consider the pinnacle of Sumerian political and cultural achievement: the Akkadian Empire. We will learn the story of one of the great king of Mesopotamia - King Sargon - and we will explore the details and stories that make the Akkadian period an interesting if little known one.

Sargon of Akkad

Akkad was the name of both a city and a region. It is important to remember that in these early days of Mesopotamia, and even later, cities lay at the center of both religious and political life. The city-state was the main polity of Mesopotamia, and it would continue to be important off and on for millennia, although the rise of empires like the Akkadian, Babylonian, and Assyrian would buck this city-state emphasis somewhat. In this respect, Sumerian history does seem to bear some resemblance to later Greek history. In Greece, too, the citystate political unit eventually gave way to larger kingdoms and empires, such as that of Macedon and the Seleucids.

Sargon was, therefore, born into a complex political web that included independent city-states and non-Sumerian peoples living in close proximity to the Sumerians. For example, the name Akkad is of non-Sumerian origin which would seem to indicate that at least some of the peoples in Mesopotamia at this time, if not the Akkadians themselves, were not only not Sumerian but perhaps not even Mesopotamian. The city of Akkad was located in the plain between the Tigris and Euphrates rivers, although its exact location has not been positively identified.

Sargon began his state by defeating the city-state of Uruk, which was headed by a ruler called Lugal-zage-si. Lugal-zagesi is believed to be the only king of the Third Dynasty of Uruk, which was perhaps the most important of the Sumerian citystates at this time. Sargon conquered the state of Lugal-zagesi, which includes smaller cities.

Sargon himself was of humble origins. Sargon, whose name means "the legitimate king" was the son of a gardener called Itti-Bel or La'ibum. His mother was believed to be a hierodule to the goddess Inanna (or Ishtar). A hierodule was a sacred prostitute who served the goddess in various ways in her temple. Another myth states that Sargon's mother was a changeling while he did not know his father. This legend states that Sargon's mother became pregnant and places him in a basket and sent him down the river. He was found by a man whose job it was to draw water from the river. This man reared Sargon, eventually making him his gardener. Sargon's genealogy would later be elaborated to give his forebears a veneer of nobility, one which they had not possessed in the earliest accounts.

We do know that Sargon started out his career as a cupbearer to the king of Kish, an important city-state. This king was called Ur-Zababa, and Sargon later displaced him. In fact, the position of cupbearer was apparently of high importance at the time as it placed its holder in close proximity to the king. Sargon would go on to reign for 45 years according to a cuneiform account. The generally accepted account is that he actually reigned for 56 years. During this time, he greatly enlarged his empire. For instance, King Sargon invaded the region of Canaan and Syria four times.

The single most important accomplishment of Sargon was that he united the city-states of Sumer and Akkad for the first time. This made Mesopotamia into a political and economic center without peer. Trade flourished in the region. Silver from Asia Minor and cedar from Lebanon were traded with lapis lazuli from the highlands of modern-day Afghanistan and copper from Phoenicia. The backbone of the economy was the agricultural produce that came from Assyria, which lay to the north of Sumer.

Monumental images of Sargon were erected throughout Mesopotamia, even on the eastern shores of the Mediterranean Sea. Sargon extended his control beyond Mesopotamia and the Eastern Mediterranean. He conquered the regions of Elam and Subartu. In the records that he created to his accomplishments (on his monuments), Sargon boasted of having conquered the four quarters, which included Sumer, Assyria, Elam, and Martu. It has been suggested that this king rebuilt the city of Babylon, though it would have been only a small settlement at this time.

Unification of Akkadians and Sumerians

In terms of religion, the Sargonic period was a time of unification in more ways than one. Of course, the Sumerians and Akkadians now found themselves politically unified, but there also began a period of cultural and religious syncretism that would continue over hundreds of years. This process would be so complete that eventually, Sumerian would find itself replaced by Akkadian and other non-Sumerian languages. But Sargon was smart enough not to alienate the Sumerian people religiously. He paid special attention to honoring Zababa and Inanna, who were two important gods of the Sumerians. Inanna was the highly worshipped queen of heaven and the patroness of Sargon, while Zababa was the warrior divinity of the city of Kish.

The unification begun by Sargon would be fraught with difficulty. These difficulties appeared both during Sargon's own life as well as during the reigns of his successors. Numerous kings rebelled against him and formed coalitions. Sargon did experience success in defeating his rivals again and again during his lifetime. Rimush and Manishtushu were sons of Sargon who became kings after him. They both had to fight wars against rebels who sought to bring down the empire their father had built. The Akkadian Empire experienced a revival of sorts during the reign of a son of Manishtushi, Naram-Sin, who defeated his revivals and continued the process of religious, economic, and political unification then taking place in Mesopotamia. It would be about 100 years after NaramSin's death that the Akkadian Empire would collapse, ushering in a dark age for Mesopotamia. At this time, the government of the region reverted to that of local city-states competing against each other and vying for influence.

The Marriage of Martu

The Marriage of Martu is a tale from the Akkadian period or immediately after. It has been dated to the period between about 2200 BC and 2000 BC. This is a tale of Martu and his romance with a princess. Martu was another name for Amurru who would become the patron deity of the Amorites who created the Babylonian Empire. In the story, Martu is described as a warrior. It was not uncommon for deities in these early tales to be described as if they were ordinary people even though they would be worshipped by devotees in the region.

Martu travels to the city in search of a bride for himself. He sees a beautiful princess and she notices him, as well. He wins the hand of the princess by besting a foe in a wrestling competition. He satisfies the family of the princess by bringing them gifts. The princess's father gives his blessing to the union. An observer points out that Martu, as a nomad from outside the city, appears uncivilized but the princess does not care about this. There are a number of important themes in

the Marriage of Martu. One of them is that love conquers all, but another is the important relationship between city dwellers and rural folk. There was a need for them to find common ground if they were going to work together in the empires that were taking shape in the region.

Chapter 11: Twenty Essential Facts about Sumerian History and Mythology

Fact One. Sumerian civilization is the oldest known civilization in the world.

Sumer was remarkable not just for its achievements. Sumer was remarkable for being able to concentrate so many great achievements into a single place and time. The historical record tells us that the Sumerians were the oldest civilization, even older than the Egyptians. Of course, being the first civilization, the Sumerians lived in large urban settlements where they built grand edifices called ziggurats. Early Sumerian cities made great advancement that remain with us to the present.

Fact Two. Sumer lies in an important geographic region known as Mesopotamia.

Mesopotamia means the land between the rivers. Sumer lay in the southern part of Mesopotamia, which was a highly fertile land because it lay between these two rivers and the land was flat and well-watered: perfectly suited for farmland or grazing land. The rivers that the Mesopotamian land lies between were the Tigris River and Euphrates River. Today, most of Mesopotamia lies in the modern nation of Iraq, although there are parts also in Kuwait, Turkey, and Syria.

Fact Three. The transition of humans from huntergathering to large scale agriculture is believed to have occurred at Sumer.

It is easy to take civilization for granted because it has been around for long. If you lived in ancient Sumer, you would not have taken civilized life for granted. You would have seen all around you the clear difference between life in cities and life outside of them. The Sumerians even told stories about men who learned first-hand about these differences. The main advancement that allowed men to live in cities was the development of large-scale agricultural practices. The transition to this type of practice began here, which is why civilization also began here.

Fact Four. The oldest writing system in the world was developed at Sumer.

The Sumerians had many stories about how writing began. One involved a king who had to deal with the frequent messages that he had to send back and forth with another king. In reality, language probably developed because life in cities would have required a way for people to communicate quickly and efficiently without the need for spoken messages that might be lost in the retelling.

Fact Five. Many common elements of math and timekeeping come from the Sumerians.

The Sumerians are responsible for a number of important advancements in mathematics and astronomy. This included the sixty-second minute as well as the sixty-minute hour. They even divided the year into twelve parts just as we do today.

Fact Six. The Sumerian pantheon numbered between one hundred and three hundred gods.

The Sumerians worshipped a large number of gods. There are a number of interesting reasons for this. One reason is that each city-state had their patron deity who they built a large temple for and there were a lot of cities. Another reason was that as city-states became empires, all these different gods became united in a single pantheon.

Fact Seven. Over time, the people of Mesopotamia amalgamated both in terms of language and religious practice.

One of the most interesting periods in Sumerian history is the Akkadian. The Akkadian period was notable for the amalgamation of two distinct cultures: that of Akkad and that of Sumer. These groups both had their own languages and gods, and during this time, a period of cultural and religious unification began.

Fact Eight. Several empires included the region of Sumer, including the Akkadian, Hurrian, Babylonian, Assyrian, and Persian.

The Mesopotamian region was notable for the many states that created empires on its fertile plain. Although some of these empires were foreign, not all of them were. For example, the Akkadian, Assyrian, and Babylonian empires can truly be thought of as Mesopotamian states.

Fact Nine. The original political system of Sumer consisted of independent city-states.

The city-state was the original political unit of Sumer. It makes sense as civilization implies city living, and you have to start with cities before you get to empires. Even thousands of years later, the city remained the basic political unit of Mesopotamia.

Fact Ten. It is believed that many of the heroes of Sumer like Gilgamesh, Lugalbanda, and Atrahasis began as historical kings.

What is interesting about mythology is that, often, you find that the heroes of myth were actually real people. Historians believe that Gilgamesh, Lugalbanda, and Atrahasis were real kings who lived in Sumer. Sargon is another example of a king whose life became obscured by myth.

Fact Eleven. Sumerian mythology and history probably share the most in common with the Norse in terms of major belief systems.

The Norse were other people who placed emphasis on heroes and histories as well as tales of gods and men. Indeed, the Norse sagas are really the tales of heroes, many of whom were real men. In this regard, Sumer has quite a lot in common with the Norse. It can also be said that the Sumerians share some commonality with the Greeks, too. The Greeks also placed a lot of emphasis on heroes, although the dividing line between the hero and the god was very distinct in Greek myth and much less so for the Sumerians.

Fact Twelve. The position of chief god in the Sumerian pantheon changed over time.

An interesting fact about the Sumerians is that they did not have a stable chief god throughout their history. Sometimes, their chief god was Enlil; sometimes, it was Enlil or Anu, yet other times, it was Marduk, Ashur, Nanna, or Inanna. This is quite singular in history, though it reflects the reality both of Sumerian politics and the shifting status of Mesopotamia in terms of the ruler. Because each city had its god, as one city rose so too did its god. This pattern was replicated later as empires replaced city-states. When an empire rose, it promoted its own god.

Fact Thirteen. Each empire that existed in Mesopotamia promoted a new chief god compared to the empire that had come before.

The Babylonians promoted Marduk as their god, while the

Assyrians promoted their eponymous god Ashur. These gods supplanted the earlier chief gods like Enlil and An that had been significant in the region.

Fact Fourteen. All of the gods of Sumer were believed to be descended from An (or Anu) who was the god of the sky.

The gods of Sumer were sometimes referred to as the Anunnaki. This was a pantheon that reflected their descent from the god of the sky (or the heavens), An. The Sumerians believed that life began in the form of cosmic births. The god Enlil was born to the sky, An, and the earth, Ki. Enlil later supplanted Ki to be the god of the earth.

Fact Fifteen. Inanna was the longest lasting of the Sumerian gods, being worshipped as late as the 18th century of our era.

Inanna truly was a fascinating goddess. She was called Queen of Heaven and Lady of Earth. She was the sister of the goddess of the underworld, Ereshkigal. Importantly, Inanna was also the goddess of love and a goddess of war. She must have had some appeal if she lasted as long as she did: literally outlasting all of the other gods.

Fact Sixteen. Inanna was introduced into Greek mythology as Aphrodite.

Greek historians understood that Aphrodite had not originated with their people. She had come to the Greeks as Ashtoreth, a Phoenician goddess. She had come through trade at Phoenician (and Greek ports). But Ashtoreth was none other than Inanna, or Ishtar, an old and powerful Sumerian goddess.

Fact Seventeen. Lugalbanda was a king of Sumer who was believed to have reigned for 1200 years.

The line between hero and god was a little blurred in Sumerian myth. Sumerian tales told of how kings sometimes asked to be inducted as gods. They were generally refused, although that did not stop them from reigning for hundreds of years, just as if they had been gods. Lugalbanda is a good example of this theme.

Fact Eighteen. The Sumerian fondness for beer was embodied in a goddess of theirs called Ninkasi, the goddess of beer.

Many Sumerian stories talk about the drinking of beer or about a particular character's fondness for beer. Well, it should come as no surprise that the Sumerians had a god of beer: Ninkasi. Many Sumerian myths descend into meanderings about the beauty of a city or its great monuments; or about the greatness of a temple or the god that it belonged to. Well, some tales even start going on about beer. Go figure.

Fact Nineteen. The Sumerians used cuneiform writing for more than three thousand years, right up until the time of Jesus.

What is interesting about Sumerian cuneiform writing is that they continued to use it, and versions of it, right up until the end of their civilization. And they did this even though new forms of writing that must have been easier to use had been invented. This is not hard to understand when one keeps in mind the religious significance of the writing and the importance of preserving this religious writing in its original form.

Fact Twenty. Sumerian history was lost until about 200 years ago. Now, we have been able to reconstruct Sumerian history with the aid of 500,000 tablets that have been found (some have yet to be translated).

The deciphering of clay tablets has allowed us to understand the Sumerian world with some rapidity. It boggles the mind to think, too, that there are hundreds of thousands of tablets yet to be deciphered. One can only imagine what amazing things there are to learn.

List of Sumerian Gods, Goddesses, and Heroes

The Sumerian pantheon was filled with gods, goddesses, demons, and monsters totaling more than three hundred in number. Many gods became syncretized over time or saw their names changed. For example, Inanna saw her cult increase greatly over time and was generally known as Ishtar in Babylon and Ashtoreth in Phoenicia. Even the chief deities of the Sumerians changed. At one moment, it was Enlil, at another An, and at other moments, Ashur or Marduk. Here we provide a reference to the major gods, goddesses, and other characters of Sumerian myth.

Chief Deities:

Enlil (or Ellil): the Great Mountain, Lord of the Wind, Father of the Gods

Anu (or An): god of the sky

Enki: god of wisdom, water, and creation; ruler of the Earth

Other Deities:

Adad: god of storms

Amurru: god of nomads and Lord of the Mountain; eponymous god of the Amorites

Anzu: a giant bird who steals the Tablet of Destinies

Apkallu: One of seven sages or wise men of Babylonian myth

Ashur: The main god of the Assyrian people; sometimes shown riding a snake

Bull of Heaven: character who appears in the Epic of Gilgamesh; Inanna convinces her father Anu to unleash the Bull of Heaven against Gilgamesh

Ea: god of the waters upon which Earth is floating

Ereshkigal: goddess of the underworld; sister to Inanna, Queen of Heaven

Gula: goddess of doctors and healing

Inanna or Ishtar: goddess of love, war, and fertility

Lama: goddess of personal or private protection (the same as Lamassu, but depicted as female)

Lamassu: a bull or lion with a human head

Lamashtu: a demon that preys on children

Mami: a mother goddess from the Epic of Atrahasis

Marduk: protector god of Babylon

Martu: an alternative name for Amurru, the eponymous god of the Amorites

Mushhushshu: a furious snake or dragon that serves as protector of the other gods of the Sumerian pantheon

Nabu: patron of writing and god of scribes

Nanna: god of wisdom and the moon; also known as Sin

Nergal: god of the underworld; husband to Ereshkigal

Ninhursag: mother goddess of Sumer

Ninurta: god of war

Nanna: god of wisdom and the moon

Pazuzu: the demonic god who protects human beings from evil forces and pestilence

Scorpion People: servants of the god Shamash (or Utu-Shamash)

Sin: a moon god

Tiamat: a goddess of anger who fought against the gods and was often depicted as a dragon or a giant sea serpent; the Tigris and Euphrates flow from her cut in half body

Ugallu: a demon with the head of a lion, body of a human, and feet of a bird; protects human beings from illness **Usmu**: messenger god and god of the city of Ea

Utu-Shamash (or Shamash): God of the sun; brother to Inanna.

Main Heroes:
Enmerkar: a king who was said to rule between 420 and 900 years

Etana: the legendary king of the city of Kish

Gilgamesh: hero from the Epic of Gilgamesh; also a historical king of the city of Uruk.

Utnapishtum: a hero from the book the Epic of Gilgamesh; said to be an ancestor of Gilgamesh

Frequently Asked Questions

1. Who were the Sumerians?

The Sumerians were the people of Sumer, a region in Mesopotamia. Mesopotamia was the area between two rivers, namely the Tigris River and the Euphrates River. This region is located mostly in Iraq, although there are portions of it also in Syria, Turkey, and Kuwait. This region was highly fertile and the Sumerians lived in the southernmost aspect of it. The Sumerians spoke a non-Semitic language and wrote in a cuneiform script that was also of non-Semitic origin.

The place and even the definition of Sumerians began to change during the Akkadian period. The Sumerian period technically lasted nearly 2000 years, beginning in about 4000 or 4500 BC. The Sumerians eventually were superseded by a people called the Akkadians who lived immediately to the north of Sumer. The Sumerian language had to compete with the Akkadian language, which caused the people of the Akkadian Empire (who controlled both Akkad and Sumer) to be mostly bilingual.

2. What was significant about the Sumerian period?

The Sumerians were significant for a number of reasons. For one thing, many of the advancements that we associate with modern life originated with the Sumerians. Much of our understanding of mathematics, astrology, and accounting comes from the Sumerians. The Sumerians divided the minute into sixty seconds and the hour into sixty minutes. They divided the year into divisions of twelve and used the constellations in the sky to tell time and make predictions about the weather.

But perhaps, the single most important fact to know about the Sumerians and the period in which they lived is that the Sumerians are generally regarded to be the first civilization in the world. Indeed, it can be said that they invented civilized life. Because they were Masters of Agriculture, people no longer had to spend their time looking for food or dealing with other concerns of survival. A small number of people could handle the needs of feeding the population while others can be evolved in other matters. There could be no tradesmen without the agricultural advancements of the Sumerians. Indeed, there could be no mathematicians and scientists without the farmers who carried the weight of feeding the population on their shoulders. We have the Sumerians to thank for this change in the way humans live.

3. Were the Sumerians and the Akkadians distinct peoples?

It is not always easy to understand who ancient peoples truly were or where they came from. For example, to this day, historians are not entirely clear who the Ancient Egyptians "were" or where they came from. They spoke a Semitic language that was distinct from other Semitic languages. Did they come from the Near East, Africa, or both? These sorts of questions are very difficult to answer because our understanding of nationality and ethnicity is just that: modern. The people of the past were not as "pure" as people of today like to think they are in their own groups. Most peoples were actually a mélange of the many different peoples who passed through the region.

Of course, this does not answer the question about the Sumerians and the Akkadians so we will give that one a go, too. The Sumerians and Akkadians were distinct people. The Sumerians spoke a distinct language from the Akkadians. They lived in distant regions, as well, even though both Sumer and Akkad are now within the modern nation of Iraq and are now longer culturally or ethnically distinct. Much has been said about the bilingualism of the Akkadian Imperial Period, which attests to the fact that Akkad and Sumer were originally distinct until political concerns eventually caused an amalgamation of these people, a phenomenon that would continue to be common in Mesopotamia.

4. What language was spoken during the Akkadian period?

During the Akkadian period, two languages were spoken. There was the original Sumerian language, which had its own form of writing. And there was also the Akkadian language, which was a distinct language with its own separate way of writing. Because Akkadian could not supplant Sumerian in the early years due to the religious and cultural importance of Sumerian, many people at the time would have been bilingual in Sumerian and Akkadian; at least this is what historians today believe. As the cultures and gods syncretized, Sumerian as a language would eventually disappear.

5. Who were the Amorites and why were they important?

The Amorites were a Semitic people whose lands lay outside of Mesopotamia. Specifically, they lived on the "steppes" and mountainsides to the West of Sumer, therefore along the Eastern Mediterranean Sea. The Amorites have been coopted by theorists with various agendas over the years, but today we know that they were a clearly Semitic people who perhaps were identical to the Canaanites who dwelled in the region of the Southern Levant before the arrival of the Jews from Egypt.

Amurru was the name for both a specific people (who we now know today as the Amorites) and for the god that they worshipped. This god was also called Martu, and his important city was called Ninab. Like many other cities of the region, the precise location of this city is not known to historians and archaeologists. Amurru and Martu are documented in texts in both the Akkadian and Sumerian languages.

Amurru was regarded as the god of the Amorite people. The Amorites were originally a tribal, uncivilized people who lived on the fringe of the Akkadian and Neo-Sumerian empires. They were pastoral and they were often referred to as people of the mountain or of the steppe. For this reason, Amurru (the god) was also referred to as lord of the mountain or lord of the steppe.

6. Who was the chief god of the Sumerians?

This is not a simple question to answer. Indeed, this is a trickier question to answer for the Sumerians than it would be for the Greeks, Romans, or the Norse. The Greeks had Zeus and the Norse had Odin. Simple enough. But for the

Sumerians, the chief gods changed depending on which rulers were in power and which city was the center of the civilization.

Enlil is generally regarded as the chief Sumerian god, but properly that is only true of the early civilization of Sumer and the Akkadian period. Even during this time, gods like An or Enki rivaled Enlil in importance or even surpassed him. For the Assyrians and the Assyrian period in Sumer, Ashur was the supreme deity. During the Babylonian period, the chief god would have been Marduk. Over time, Inanna grew in importance until she became perhaps the most worshipped divinity in Mesopotamia. As you can see, the Mesopotamians did not really have a Zeus or an Odin who occupied a stable place in their civilization. Their pantheon was constantly opening itself to new gods, and the chief god was adapted to fit the rulers who controlled Sumer and what their chief city (and divinity) was.

7. Are Mesopotamian divinities referenced outside the region of Mesopotamia?

A number of Sumerian divinities were referenced in the records of neighboring regions. In some cases, they were adapted to be gods of these regions while in others they were mentioned as being in conflict with local gods or local people. For example, the Bible and Talmud reference a number of foreign deities, including Sumerian ones. Ba'al was a Canaanite god, but his name merely meant "lord" and several Mesopotamian gods might have been equated with Ba'al. Nergal is an interesting divinity because of references made to him outside of Mesopotamia.

Nergal was a god of the underworld. He was described in many myths as the consort of Ereshkigal, who was the ruler of the underworld and the sister of Inanna, the Queen of Heaven. Nergal's seat of worship was at the city of Cuthah, also known as Cuth. Nergal was worshipped very late in the period, with some of the most striking imagery of him coming from the Parthians. The Parthians ruled a large multi-ethnic empire from about 200 BC to about 200 AD.

Nergal was mentioned in the Bible as the patron divinity of the city of Cuth, which is usually known today as Cuthah. The Babylonian equivalent of Nergal, according to the Bible, was Succoth-benoth. Talmudic scholars say that the name Nergal meant "dunghill rooster" and that the symbol of Nergal was the cockerel. Nergal usually associated with the lion as his emblem. Nergal was described as being the son of Ninlil and Enlil. His siblings were Ninurta and Nanna.

8. Was Sumerian mythology confined to Mesopotamia?

Mesopotamia was a region that not only bordered many different significant people but also contained a number of people who would form empires of their own over the centuries. The Sumerians and the Akkadians were two of the important groups within Mesopotamia, but there was also the Assyrians, Hurrians, Chaldeans (Babylonians) and others. Part of what makes this picture so complicated is that some of the later peoples, like the Babylonians, were likely amalgams of earlier peoples that had been in the region. So the rise of Babylon was associated with the Amorite people who did not actually hail from Mesopotamia but from Canaan/Phoenicia. The Amorites are unlikely to have totally replaced the people who lived in Babylon and other cities of Sumer and Akkad, so the later Babylonians were probably a result of intermarriage between Sumerians, Akkadians, Amorites, Assyrians, and whomever else happened to be in the region. Historians attempt to distinguish between so-called Indo-Iranian and Indo-European people in Mesopotamia, but this is a discussion that really descends into semantics. Some historians even study the Neanderthal remains of the region and try to make associations about that lineage.

Sumerian mythology was not confined to Mesopotamia. But, as we have seen, the picture of who were Mesopotamians and who was not was complicated by waves of invasion and settlement. Remember that Mesopotamia is not only a fertile region, but one which straddles the continents of Asia,

Europe, and Africa. The Mesopotamian gods easily flowed out of Mesopotamia. Of course, the most obvious example of this was Inanna-Ishtar-Ashtoreth, but there were others as well.

9. What was the timeline of Sumerian civilization and mythology?

The timeline of Sumerian civilization and mythology was very long and complex. The first twitches of Sumerian civilization began more than 6000 years ago. Sumerian civilization began as city-states where one patron deity (or a few) were worshipped. As Sumerian civilization became more developed, and the city-state polity began to be replaced with empires - first the Akkadian, then the Babylonian, Assyrian, and others - the gods began to become part of larger and larger pantheons. So, the handful of gods of the city-states eventually gave way to the pantheon of more than 300 gods of the empires of later Mesopotamia.

Civilization in the region of Sumer can be said to have lasted right up until the rise of Islam. We can put a marker at the Islamization of the region as the end of the mythology because this was when gods like Inanna would stop being worshipped. Indeed, Mesopotamian gods had such a strong pull that many of them were worshipped in Persia and are sometimes mislabeled as Persian gods. It is tempting to try and compare the Sumerian story with that of the Greeks or even the Norse of northernmost Europe. Even compared to these elaborate mythologies, Sumerian mythology stands out as a singular and exhausting. Even the list of the most important deities changed over time, something which cannot be said of the Greeks or Norse.

10. Why did civilization begin in Mesopotamia?

There are several reasons why civilization began in Mesopotamia. In fact, the first academic exercise here is to acknowledge that most of the evidence that we have today points to Mesopotamia as the cradle of civilization, a designation that the region has had for literally thousands of years. Of course, we will never know if civilization began somewhere else, but that area is so buried beneath cities or oceans that it has no remains. If you watch a lot of cable television, you may even believe that civilization began on another planet and was brought here by aliens.

But back to Mesopotamia. Civilization began in Mesopotamia because: (1) the fertile location was perfect for agriculture; (2) ample supplies of fresh water from two rivers allowed a large population to be supported; (3) advanced agricultural technologies allowed labor to be allocated to areas outside of, well, agriculture; (4) Mesopotamia's central location likely allowed for an exchange of ideas that led to the development of civilization, as opposed to the case in more isolated areas.

11. What are the unique aspects of Sumerian religion?

Sumerian religion was unique in that many gods had anthropomorphic qualities. Gods may be depicted with the bodies of animals. They may have the wings of an animal attached to their bodies. Or they might have the feet of a bird. Sumerian religion was also unique because of the extent to which syncretism saw different gods combined as time went on. This meant that in many ways, Sumerian religion was constantly changing. Unlike in Greece where the relationship between the gods was relatively fixed, in Sumerian religion, the gods' relationships towards one another might change. The name and identity of a god's wife may change, or one god may find himself the son of a different god than he had been before.

It is also interesting to point out that some of the myths about Sumerian gods speak of them as if they were ordinary people that had lived or kings. They may be described as nomads who travel from this place to that. Or as kings who visit cities, people, and other places. This suggests that perhaps some of the Sumerian gods were men and women who became immortalized through myth. Another theory is that it was important to the Sumerians to see their gods as being like themselves in some way.

12. Can the gods of Mesopotamia be equated with Egyptian, Greek, or Roman gods?

It is difficult to create a system that aligns the gods of Mesopotamia with the gods of other mythologies like the Greeks or the Egyptians. Mesopotamian gods were not only distinct from the gods of other pantheons, but they were in a constant state of flux. The chief Sumerian deity was not consistent throughout the Sumerian period so we cannot say, for example, Enlil was the chief Sumerian god so he should be equated with Zeus, et cetera. Enlil was chief of the pantheon for a time, but at later times, the chief gods were An (or Anu), Marduk, Ashur, and even Inanna.

13. Did any of the gods of Mesopotamia make it into other major mythologies?

It has been argued that some of the male Mesopotamian gods may have infiltrated into the pantheons of other peoples, including the Phoenicians and even the Greeks. It becomes difficult at times to equate one good with another even in this context because of confusion about names or titles. For example, the title Ba'al, which means lord, was used to refer to multiple different Mesopotamian deities. A prominent example of a deity that made it into several other pantheons, however, is Inanna, who was known by a different name depending on who worshipped her.

14. Ishtar seems to be the most famous of the Sumerian or Mesopotamian gods and goddesses. Why is that?

Ishtar seems to fill a need that existed in the Near East and other regions. Ishtar, or more properly, Inanna, was a goddess with a strong sensual element. She not only was a goddess of love, sex, and desire, but she was even a goddess of warfare. There is imagery in which Ishtar, or Inanna, is shown brandishing weapons in order to lead armies into war. All the while, she might be wearing a skirt that prominently displays her legs or the sensuality of her body.

It seems fitting that the Greeks would adopt a version of Ishtar into their pantheon. This, of course, was Aphrodite, who took on an important role as a goddess of love for the Greeks. She appeared in several significant stories, including that of the Judgment of Paris and the Trojan War. Interestingly enough,

Aphrodite in Greek myth usually was not associated with war.

It seems that this version of a strongly sensual goddess may have been a little more than the Greeks could tolerate. Whatever the case may be, Ishtar seemed to benefit not only from the prominence of the role which she filled but from the importance of cities like Babylon and others where she was highly valued.

15. **Sometimes, gods and characters of mythology actually turn out to be real. Were any characters from Sumerian myth real?**

This is another interesting question. The prevalence of shared names among the gods and the king lists suggests that either some of the gods were real kings that lived, or the kings took their name from the gods. Another option is that mythological stories were created to glorify the kings who ruled important cities. This seems to be the case in the myth of Atrahasis as Atrahasis has been shown to be a king of an important Sumerian city in an early period.

16. Why is it important to understand the history of Sumer when studying Sumerian mythology?

One of the more remarkable aspects of Sumerian mythology is that there were constantly more gods being added to the pantheon. Also, the role of this god might change. Getting a little bit of knowledge about Sumerian history allows you to understand why one god increased the importance of a period of several centuries while another god declined. We have already seen how Enlil and Anu experienced a relative decline in their significance, relinquishing much of their position to regional deities like Ashur, Marduk, Amurru, and others. This discussion forms a nice caveat to the next question.

17. Why were Sumerian gods and goddesses primarily associated with cities?

Sumer and Mesopotamia were a region of large cities. They should more properly be called city-states because, in the early history of Mesopotamia, these large cities held sway over surrounding swathes of territory. These cities had their own gods that they patronized. These gods were closely associated with the fortunes of the city. If a city was successful, it was believed that it was due to the intercession of the god. If the god failed, it could be interpreted as the god had abandoned the city or the god was weak.

This sort of civic idea seemed to be deeply held in the region of the Near East. Even in the Bible, there are references to the God of Israel being greater than this god or that. This reflects a belief that was held then that the god was the embodiment of the strength and vitality of the people. And as the people of early Mesopotamia were grouped into city-states, this meant that the gods advocated for cities. Cities built large, elaborate temples for their god. If a particular city founded an empire by conquering other cities, that god of a city would become a major god of the pantheon while still being associated with a particular place.

18. Is Anu the equivalent of Zeus? If not, who is?

Anu, or An, was a sky god. It is tempting to equate Anu with Zeus, but one has to be careful not to be led astray here. Although Anu was one of the Seven Great Gods of Sumer (and even one of the three primary gods), Enlil was frequently perceived as being more central and important in myth than Anu. For this reason, equating Anu with Zeus becomes difficult as Zeus was king of the gods. Anu and Enlil both fathered other gods so one might say that as All-Father or leader of the pantheon, Enlil is more suitable than Anu. Anu might even be seen as a sort of Cronus: leader of the Titans and father of Zeus.

19.   Why is Sumerian mythology so little known compared to the mythologies of other regions?

One of the reasons for this is the relative complexity of Sumerian gods. There were hundreds of them and their roles in Sumerian life changed across the ages. Ishtar (or Inanna) is known to many today because her name sometimes crops up in school lessons, but most of the Sumerian gods are unknowns. Another reason for the obscurity of Sumerian mythology is that these gods are very far removed from modern life both culturally and in terms of time. They do not generally appear in Western movies, television shows, or books so they come across as strange and fascinating.

20.   What impact has Ancient Sumerian civilization had on life today?

Many advancements of the Sumerian period we take advantage of today. Historians hold the Sumerians responsible for the sixty-second minute, the sixty-minute hour, the year divided neatly into twelve months, and even the modern practice of extensive agricultural production. Indeed, there were no cities before the Sumerians because the Sumerian people of Mesopotamia were the inventors of civic life. They were the first to live in cities and they were the first to live in the city-state as a political unit. It is difficult to imagine what our world would like if it had not been for the Sumerians and all that they contributed to the way in which human beings interact with their world.

21. How did Mesopotamian gods and goddesses spread to other regions?

Mesopotamia was an important region for a number of reasons. In addition to being the originator of a number of practices and technologies that spread to other areas, Mesopotamia was also strategically placed. Herein lies one of the great draws to the region both to local kings and outside conquerors. Mesopotamia divided the Western portion of the Near East from Egypt and the Mediterranean Sea. This meant that invaders from Persia or Parthia, for example, needed to cross through this region to reach their likely destinations. This is part of the way in which Mesopotamian gods and goddesses spread to other regions. Contact of strategically located Mesopotamia with regions like Phoenicia and Persia allowed Mesopotamian ideas to spread to these areas. This contact may have been in the form of trade or it may have been by conquest. For example, Mesopotamian gods likely spread to Persia after Babylon and its empire was conquered by Persia.

At the same time, it is known that gods like the Phoenician Ashtoreth (who was based on Inanna/Ishtar) spread to Greece to become Aphrodite through trade.

22. What was hieros gamos and why was it important?

Hieros gamos is actually a Greek word that refers to a sacred marriage. This was a marriage in which opposite principles of male and female were combined to give birth to cosmic life. This belief is another example of a Sumerian cosmic principle, but it also underlies the union of An and Ki to give birth to Enlil and subsequently life. The tale of Enki and Ninhursag, which will be related shortly, explains how Enki is living with his wife in Dimun, which is a paradise. Enki is lord of Ab, which means fresh water, but which ca1n also refer to male semen.

The idea of the sacred marriage actually exists in other cultures outside of Mesopotamia. In Hinduism, there was a ritual where girls were dedicated to a temple, which was perceived as a sort of marriage to the god that involved dance and other rituals. For the Greeks, the marriage of Zeus and Hera was the most important sacred marriage, and this would have been reenacted at ceremonies, especially on the island of Samos where the marriage was said to take place. In Sumer, it was important that the kings undertake a sacred marriage to the priestess of Inanna, representing the union from which the life and welfare of the people in the city-state would spring.

23. What was the Atra-Hasis in Sumerian myth?

Atrahasis, or the Epic of Atrahasis, is the most complete account of the Great Flood in Mesopotamian literature. The tale was adapted as a part of the Epic of Gilgamesh though some of the characters' names were altered. The Atrahasis (also Atra-Hasis) was written during the Akkadian period. Recall that the Akkadians were the people dwelling to the immediate north of the Sumerians proper. During the Akkadian period, which began with King Sargon, the Akkadians and Sumerians were unified into a single state known as the Akkadian Empire.

The Epic of Atrahasis was written around 1800 BC. It was recorded in the Semitic Akkadian language upon clay tablets. The name indicated that the contents of the tablets contained great wisdom. The contents included a Sumerian creation story as well as the story of the Great Flood. Atrahasis was not only the name for this work. The name also appears on the Sumerian King List, meaning that it indicates a king of a

Sumerian city-state; in this case, the city of Shuruppak. This king lived in antediluvian times. The Atrahasis begins with events antecedent to the Deluge.

24. Who were the Seven Great Gods of Sumer?

The Seven Great Gods of Sumer were counted as An, Enlil, Enki, Utu, Inanna (or Ishtar), Ninhursag, and Nanna. Although sometimes used as a synonymous term with Annunaki, Igigi in the Epic of Atrahasis referred to the lesser gods who were servants to the Seven Great Gods.

25. Who was the greatest Sumerian hero?

The greatest Sumerian hero was certainly Gilgamesh. Like many of the Greek heroes, such as Theseus, Gilgamesh was a real person who reigned as king of a Sumerian city-state. Like Theseus, Sumerian acquired demigod status as the centuries went on. Gilgamesh was the ruler of the city of Uruk, one of the most important cities of Sumer. Gilgamesh was the hero of the Epic of Gilgamesh, which was actually a series of poems. These poems were written at different dates, and some poems are in a better state of preservation than others. It is believed that the earliest of these poems was Gilgamesh, Enkidu, and the Netherworld. This is the poem where Gilgamesh sends scurrying the creatures surrounding Inanna's huluppu tree. After the death of Enkidu, Gilgamesh learns of the conditions in the "Netherworld."

The Epic of Gilgamesh was composed of separate poems about the life of Gilgamesh. The formal epic was written by a scribe called Sin-leqi-unninni around 1600 BC, but it was based on the epic poems that had been written earlier. Gilgamesh of the epic was a demigod who has dealings with Inanna (known at the time the epic was written as Ishtar). The real Gilgamesh was a king who lived sometime between 2900 BC and 2300 BC. This would place him just before the foundation of the Akkadian Empire by King Sargon. Although there are no remains from Gilgamesh's reign, a monument from the reign of King Ishbi-Erra of Sumer credits Gilgamesh with erecting the walls of the city of Uruk. Ishbi-Erra reigned as king circa 1900 BC.

Conclusion

Sumerian mythology has been shrouded in mystery for thousands of years. Indeed, until the 18th and 19th centuries, almost nothing was known about the gods and goddesses of the Sumerian pantheon. Even less was known about their heroes. The tales of the world's first true civilization are being exposed to the light of day, enrapturing men and women worldwide. The stories of Enkidu, Nanna, Enlil, Ereshkigal, and Gilgamesh are finding new audiences, men and women curious to learn about a society very different from our own. Sumerian mythology was so powerful that some of their gods found their way into different cultures, the most famous example of this being Aphrodite who began her journey as Inanna. In *Sumerian Mythology: Fascinating Sumerian History and Mesopotamian Empire and Myths*, you learned the tales of gods and great men. These are the tales that form the canon of Sumerian religion.

Sumerian civilization has covertly become an important contributor to the manner in which we live today. Most of us are unaware of it. The way that we measure time, observe the stars, and even plant and grow crops has a lot to do with the advancements made by the Sumerians more than six thousand years ago. Also, it was heroes like Gilgamesh who have helped define what it means to be a hero in today's world. These heroes were men who became gods, earning their place in the stars in more ways than one. The Sumerians used their tales as instructions for others in how to live and even to help themselves understand their own place in the world. *Sumerian Mythology: Fascinating Sumerian History and Mesopotamian Empire and Myths* taught you the formative tales of gods and heroes to help you understand who the Sumerians were and why they were important.

Sumerian Mythology: Fascinating Sumerian History and Mesopotamian Empire and Myths explored the tales of gods and heroes. These stories of gods and heroes were deeply significant to the Mesopotamian people, and learning about them is how you came to understand the kind of world they lived in and how it was different from our own. It was a world of birds with the faces of lions, gods with the wings of birds, and seductive goddesses who symbolically married the kings of the various city-states. The Sumerians told many stories of gods like Utu, Nanna, An, Ashur, and Inanna, stories that helped the empires of Mesopotamia endure for nearly 4000 years. In fact, European travelers to the Near East in the 18th century discovered that there were still districts where the goddess Inanna (more than five thousand years old then) was still worshipped in secret.

The world of the Sumerians was unlike our own. The people at the heart of Sumerian civilization - living in modern-day Iraq, Kuwait, Syria, and other places - these people were part of a culture so far removed from the way that we think and perceive today as to be almost unrecognizable. *Sumerian Mythology: Fascinating Sumerian History and Mesopotamian Empire and Myths* gave you the lens through which to see their world. It was a world of great empires: the Akkadian, Hurrian, Assyrian, and Babylonian. It was a world of legendary wealth and beauty.

You began your odyssey with the Sumerians by learning about their history. Sumer was notable as being the world's oldest known civilization, experiencing dizzying heights more than one thousand years before Egypt. They built ziggurats that touched the sky and gardens that overflowed into the canals that fed their farmlands. In many ways, Sumer was a paradise. But if their gods were anything to go by, it was not always smooth sailing. In this chapter, you learned how Sumer experienced several painful periods of unification, the first one beginning with the Akkadian Empire. At this time, the long process of Akkadian replacing Sumerian as the major local language began.

Sumerian society was complex, like all societies that characterize major civilizations. At the center of the civilization was the city-state, and sitting atop the city-state were the kings and the priests. These two groups engaged in a complex dance, but it was an important one. Just as in Egypt, the rulers in Sumer understood that a stable reign required that they recognize and support religion in real ways. Perhaps, this is why the Sumerian kings created so many tablets where they boasted of building this temple or that or being in the favor of this goddess or that god. The kings of the Sumerian city-states, and the later rulers of the empires, too, symbolically married goddesses like Inanna. If that does not give you an idea of the role that religion played in their society, then nothing will.

In the third chapter, you were introduced to some of the formative myths that help set the tone for Sumerian myth. Sumerians were storytellers. They loved to extoll the strength and virtues of this hero or that king. They loved to sing the praises of this particular city or that particular temple. They were natural poets and poetic language characterizes all the tales that they told in their myths, even though we managed to distill it to solely the major points in this work. In this chapter, you learned of the Cosmic Births, the story of Enlil and Ninlil, of Enki and Ninhursag, and other tales.

In chapter four, we learned of the exploits of one of the more important characters of Sumerian myth. This character was Ninurta. We formed an idea of Ninurta and the role that he (and characters like him) played in Sumerian society (and myth). We started Ninurta's adventure off with the tale of Ninurta and Asag. We continued with the tale of Ninurta and the Turtle. And we concluded with the story of how Ninurta returned to Nippur.

Heroes serve an important role in all mythologies. They give the reader a sense of the sorts of characteristics that people in that society value. Heroes also served as a model of how people were expected to behave. Two thousand years ago, men and women will hear stories about Spider-Man, Batman, and Superman, and they will develop an idea of how we in Western society viewed the world and our place in it. In much the same way, we can read tales of Enmerkar and Sargon and learn how the Sumerians approached their world. Let us just say that these characters were very different from Spider-Man and Batman.

Inanna was one of the more important divinities in the Sumerian pantheon. She is a goddess who is easy to explore because there was just so much information about her. And we mean interesting information just as much as general information. Inanna was the Queen of Heaven. She helped men like Enmerkar, but she also had raged against heroes like Gilgamesh. She became one of the chief deities in Mesopotamia, which facilitated her being exported into Phoenicia and other areas. Through Phoenicia, she became the

Greek goddess Aphrodite. In the sixth chapter, we learned much about Inanna, including her exploits in the tales of Inanna and (Mount) Ebih, and Inanna and the Huluppu Tree.

Nanna was another very significant god. This god of the moon, at one point, became the chief deity in the Sumerian pantheon. He was said to struggle against demons who tried to steal the light of the moon, which is how lunar eclipses happened. Nanna had an important role in fertility, underlying the mysterious role that the moon played in fertility rites and the natural cycle of the earth. We learned all this and many more about Nanna in the seventh chapter. One of the tales explored here was that of Nanna's Journey to visit his father Enlil at Nippur.

The Epic of Gilgamesh is one of the most important works in the history of world literature. It is also the oldest work that still exists in nearly complete form, being written about four thousand years ago. The Epic of Gilgamesh was a compiled work of about 1800 BC that was based on much earlier epic poems about the hero Gilgamesh. There were many important stories in this epic, most of which were encapsulated in these separate poems. The tale of Gilgamesh and the ogre Huwawa, of Gilgamesh and Aga, and of Gilgamesh's meeting with the Noah of Sumer (Utnapishtum), all of these and more were explored in the eighth chapter.

Lugalbanda was an important king and hero who had several tales told about him in Sumerian myth. In the ninth chapter, we learned lighter tales of Lugalbanda in the Mountain Cave, and Lugalbanda and his dealings with the Anzu Bird: that mischievous creature that was half fowl and half lion. In the tenth chapter, we drew near a conclusion of our odyssey by exploring the Akkadian Empire, the first empire in Mesopotamia and the world. We learned of the many important trends that took place at this time, and what it meant for Sumerian history and religion. To round things up, we reviewed the gods and heroes of Sumer. The Sumerian world may have been very far removed from our own in terms of time, but in terms of the things that make us human, perhaps, they were not altogether different from us.

Manufactured by Amazon.ca
Bolton, ON